A DIALOG ON POLYGAMY

Originally Written in Italian
by Bernardino Ochino

Edited by Don Milton

All Text, Images, & Text Images Copyright 2009
Don Milton - All Rights Reserved

Editor's Dedication

To My Wife, Laura: May Our Lives Ever Be An Epic Adventure With God At The Center.

And

In Loving Memory of My Parents
Who Have Gone To Be With the Lord
Their Love for God's Word Was a Great Gift

Trust in the LORD with all thine heart;
and *lean not unto thine own understanding*.
In all thy ways *acknowledge Him,
and He shall direct thy paths*.
Proverbs 3:5-6

About Bernardino Ochino

Bernardino Ochino, the General of the order of Capuchins, first fell out of favor with Rome when he began preaching Salvation by Grace. It further came to the attention of the inquisitors that he was spouting Bible verses in the local vernacular. But Ochino did not wait for a trial, he left Italy and headed for Geneva. Shortly after his arrival, Calvin wrote well of him, "The better I learn to know the man, the more I honor him." And again, in a letter to Melancthon, "We have Bernardino Ochino of Siena here, an excellent and distinguished man." Bucer writes to Calvin, "I wish we could show Signor Bernardino the distinctions he merits, his presence is a great pleasure to us." Ochino also made his mark in England and other places and yet it is a sad fact of history that years later, when Ochino sought refuge in Germany, the surviving reformers did not welcome him but instead exiled him for his Dialog on Polygamy. Bucer and Melancthon, famous German reformers themselves, had once approved polygamy in a letter to Philip of Hesse, even attending his polygamous wedding. Yet, they had gone on to be with the Lord years earlier. The rest of Ochino's story is for another book.

About the Editor

For the last ten years, Don Milton has pastored ChristianMarriage.com, an online ministry dedicated to providing theological answers to questions about marriage. Pastor Don has published numerous books on the topics of Courtship and Christian Marriage as well as Law & Justice. He recently published his own novel, The Prince of Sumba, Husband to Many Wives, and is currently working on a historical novel. He received his Bachelor of Arts in Linguistics from the University of Washington in 1987.

Don has a wonderful wife and three children. He would like to have more.

Preface to Bernardino Ochino's

DIALOG ON POLYGAMY

Edited by Don Milton

I have in my library a copy of Select and Curious Cases of Polygamy, Concubinage, Adultery, Divorce, etc. Printed 1736. It is a small book containing some writings attributed to Bernardino Ochino of Sienna, having been translated into English. I only provide here that portion titled "On Polygamy, A Dialogue" since much of the rest of the book is either of dubious authorship or peripheral material, not written by that Great Italian Preacher, Bernardino Ochino of Sienna.

As in all restorations of old manuscripts, there are artistic decisions that must be made. I've chosen in all cases to prefer readability. You'll not find a missing letter or misplaced word within this text though the original contained both. The errors that I have found have been corrected by meticulously copying and pasting old fonts within the original images of the pages. Because of the amount of editing necessary to make the pages readable, each page is as unique as a finger print. Copyright infringers, you have been warned.

Dialog On Polygamy - Edited by Don Milton

In addition to the original translation, I've included my own modern font version which includes many editorial changes. You'll notice that I've introduced the nicknames *Ochy* and *Tely* for the characters. I find this preferable to identifying them with letters. If you're a purist, please, read the old font version. To find the old font version, open the book just beyond the middle. The pages are numbered the same in both versions to make cross referencing easier.

Had Bernardino Ochino not been exiled for writing on polygamy, he might have had more to say on the subject. Certainly there is more to say and I have done so in many of my own books. If you enjoy dialogs such as Ochino's, I've written a novel titled *Prince of Sumba, Husband to Many Wives*. Its characters argue for and against polygamy, I must admit; mostly for. It's available through most online bookstores.

I'll comment no further on this book but will allow it to speak for itself.

Don Milton

Bernardino Ochino's

DIALOG ON POLYGAMY

Edited by Don Milton

Tely. I am come to request a little of your advice; as conceiving you want neither will nor ability to afford it me: Wherefore to you it is that I choose to address myself.
Ochy. Willing I most certainly am to give it you; and also ready; provided it be nothing beyond the reach of my capacity.
Tely. What I entreat you, in the first place, is, that you faithfully-promise to keep my council.

Ochy. That you may depend on, if you advance not any thing tending to GOD'S dishonor.

Tely. I have a wife, who so little suits with my fancy, that I cannot by any means relish her; and, so far as I can hitherto perceive, she is not only barren, but unhealthy. Now, such is my disposition, that I cannot be without a woman's company; and am also desirous of having children, as well for posterity-sake, as for the pleasure I should take in educating my offspring in the fear of GOD. I might, indeed, keep a concubine, or two: But that my conscience will not suffer me to do. Nay, I might wrongfully charge my wife with adultery; and so get rid of her: But, in doing that, I should not only grievously offend the ALMIGHTY, but blemish my own and the poor woman's reputation, neither of which can I prevail with myself to offer at. One might likewise make her away by some dose: But of that I abhor even the very mention. Yet a thought is come into my head, which may make me easy; and that is, in plain terms, to marry another wife, without parting from her I have already: And this, according to my conception, GOD Himself has put into my mind, and that, by Him, I am thereunto called. My desire, therefore, is, that you will resolve me, whether according to His Word, I may not lawfully do it?

Ochy. In cases dubious, my friend, advice is very requisite. But, certainly, no case can be more evident, than that a man ought not to have more wives than one at once; the very condition of marriage being such, that it cannot be between more than two.

Tely. How is it you make that appear?

Ochy. At the beginning our Creator made, out of Adam, one woman only, and gave her to him; signifying thereby, that *he ought to have but one,* and that *matrimony ought to be but of two persons only.* Had it been his Divine pleasure, that a man should have had a plurality of women, doubtless He would have created more than one, especially in the world's infancy, when propagation was so much more necessary than for ever after.

Tely. This argument, I conceive to be but of slender validity. GOD, you say, gave to our grandsire Adam one wife; and therefore it is not lawful for any of his male posterity to have more.

Ochy. Had it been, I say again, his Creator's will, that he should have had more, He would have given him more, especially at that time of perfection in which He had vouchsafed to state him.

Tely. A mere act of GOD, without any precept thereunto annexed, does not absolutely enjoin us to a strict imitation of the same: Since, if so, we should be obliged to wear no other garments but skins, because GOD so clothed our primitive parents, and consequently our dressing ourselves in cloth, silk, etc. is unlawful. At that rate your argument would always be of force: GOD clothed them with skins, and could have clothed them with cloth, or silk, had it been His pleasure that mankind should have been so clothed. If an act of GOD does as much bind us as a precept, so that GOD'S giving to Adam one wife only was, in effect, as much as if he had said; *I will and command, that each man, shall have only one wife,* it must follow, that not only it would be illegal for a man to have more wives than one, but likewise, that every man who does not take to him a wife (having it in his power so to do) is guilty of the sin of disobedience; which is repugnant to St. Paul's Doctrine.

Ochy. You are to take notice, that the Apostle does not, in any respect, go contrary to GOD'S proceeding. GOD gave only one wife to Adam: And that was the same as if he had expressly said; *I will, that a man have not more wives than one: And it is My pleasure he shall have one, except I call him to a* *single life, by bestowing on him the Gift of Chastity.* And this is St. Paul's Intent and meaning in 1 Corinthians 7.

Tely. And I, for my part, must say, that when GOD gave to Adam one wife. it was as if He had said; *It is My pleasure, that a man shall have one wife, if either he lacks the Gift of Continence, or I shall call him to a married condition. It is also My pleasure, that he shall have no more, except he stands in need of more, or I shall call him to more.* Which is, at this present, my very condition, who stand in need of, and am called to marry another.

Ochy. That a single life is pleasing to GOD, the Word of GOD evidences: But we are not thereby taught, that He is pleased men should have more than one wife.

Tely. Nay, verily, both the Word of GOD, and the example of saints, teach the same, as shall presently be demonstrated. Meanwhile, let us, presuppose, that it had been the ALMIGHTY'S will that every man should have as many wives as he could possibly manage and govern, together with their children; how many wives must Adam have had given him, whereby to signify the Donor's pleasure, in this point?

Ochy. You are supposing what cannot be since the having more wives than one is utterly repugnant to the very essence of real matrimony.

Tely. Hitherto, you have not cleared it up to me, that the having more than one wife is repugnant to marriage, otherwise than by saying, that GOD gave to Adam one, and no more. Let us now suppose he had given him more than one. Assuredly, from that original instance you could not make good, that a man ought not to have any more than Adam had. I say, therefore, in such a case; how many wives must GOD, of necessity, have given to Adam, in order to signify the Divine pleasure, in this point?

Ochy. Two would have been very sufficient.

Tely. Now, if that act of GOD'S had been a precept, as you would urge, it would then have been unlawful for men to have had either more or less than two wives; which, nevertheless, would not have been conformable to His will, seeing His intent was, that they should have as many as they were capable of managing: Otherwise it would be sinful in a minister to celebrate the Lord's Supper, except the communicants were exactly in number so many, and no more, as were Christ's Apostles, when the same was first instituted.

Ochy. Notwithstanding, it does not necessarily follow, that, because GOD gave to Adam one wife, it is therefore unlawful for a man to have more; yet it, doubtless, is a very specious argument to persuade, nay, urges strongly, though it be not wholly compulsive.

Tely. Nay, nay; it urges not at all: Since it may be alleged, that GOD gave to Adam one wife, not to signify it to be His will, that each man should have one only wife, but rather, that all mankind in general, having proceeded as well from one mother as one father, should so much the more love and effect each other: Also that Eve, being formed of Adam's rib, might be a type of the Holy Mother Church, the only Spouse of Christ.

Ochy. Well, but let us now draw nearer to the Words of the Text. Think you not, that Adam was moved by an instinct Divine, when he said; *For this cause shall a man leave his father and mother, and cleave unto his wife*?

Tely. Doubtless he was.

Ochy. And do you not observe, that in saying, *a man shall cleave to his wife,* not *wives,* he instructs us, that a man is to have but one?

Tely. Mighty well: And, pray, when GOD commands a man to *love* his *neighbor,* does He oblige him to *love* but *one* or *more*?

Ochy. All his neighbors in general.

Tely. That is not so: For He expressly says, *Love thy neighbor,* not *thy neighbors;*

therefore, whoever loves *one* of his *neighbors,* does fulfill that injunction.

Ochy. Christ, when he said; *Love thy neighbor,* spoke it in this sense, as if he should have said; *Thou shalt* love every one of *thy* neighbors.

Tely. So likewise Adam, when he said; *He shall* cleave *unto his* wife, intimated, that he should *cleave* unto *every woman* who was *his* wife: And therefore, from those words, it cannot be made out, that it is unlawful for a man to have more than one wife.

Ochy. But what can you have to say to those words of his which follow; *And of them twain shall be made one flesh*? For he says, not of *three* or *four*. From these words it is undoubtedly manifest, that he designed not that marriage should be made between more than two persons.

Tely. Adam says not, *of them twain shall be made one flesh*; but, *They shall be made one flesh.*

Ochy. But that certainly was his meaning, as plainly appears from the Words of Christ: Who, quoting the said speech, says; That GOD, by Adam, declared, that *they two shall be one flesh*; adding this clause; They are no longer *two*, but *one* flesh.

Tely. That is, as if He had said; *The Husband shall love everyone of his wives as if she were the same flesh, and the same body* *with him;* and so, in like manner, shall every wife love her husband.

Ochy. But GOD said, *they two* shall be one; therefore *they* cannot be *three* or *four.*

Tely. Your argument would hold water, had He said, *They two only* shall be one. And so, as all this is of no force, Christ says, in Matthew 18: *If two of you, on earth, shall agree about a thing, they shall obtain what they ask.* Therefore, if three or four shall agree, they shall not obtain what they ask. So is this no sound inference. GOD said; *They* two *shall be* one *flesh*: Wherefore, if the parties be three, it is not true marriage.

Ochy. It is humanly impossible for more than *two* to become *one* flesh.

Tely. In the Primitive Church, there were not only two believers, but they were in very great numbers, having, nevertheless, but one heart, one mind: Yet you believe, that, if a man has diverse wives, he cannot become one flesh with them. *If a man, while he cleaves to a harlot, becomes,* as St. Paul says, *one body with her,* notwithstanding he has a wife, should he not much more become one flesh with her, if he makes her his wife?

Ochy. Say what you will; to have more than one wife is a thing filthy, dishonest and quite contrary, nay destructive to the holy state of matrimony.

Tely. And yet Abraham, you know, had more wives than one; as likewise David, and an abundance of others, under the Old Law. And had it been unlawful for them to have taken to them more than one wife, they would have been sinners in marrying several women; and what children they had by all their wives, except the first, would have been bastards, because not begot in lawful matrimony.

Ochy. Much sooner will I grant all this, than I will allow, or grant it to be a legal thing, for a man to entertain more than one wife. Those ancients were pious, good men, yet were they sometimes guilty of sins. They were frail sinners, as being born of Adam, as appears in the example of David: And it would have been deceiving themselves, to have denied their being sinners.

Tely. That they sometimes sinned, I shall easily grant. But I will never yield, that they continued in their sins till their death; which yet they certainly did, in case it was unlawful for them to have several wives: Whence it would follow, that they were all damned, as are those who die while they persevere in entertaining concubines. As for us, we cannot hold them for saints, since we know not, for certain, that they ever repented. David having perpetrated those sins of adultery and murder, the LORD, because he was one of his Elect, sent to him His prophet, to reprove him; as, likewise, when he numbered the people, contrary to GOD'S command. It is, therefore, very credible, that, had the having diverse wives been a breach of Divine Law, GOD would have used the like proceedings towards him, that he might have avoided eternal perdition. But peruse the Scripture throughout, yet you will not find one syllable of GOD'S having prohibited a plurality of wives: Nor is it probable that, had it been contrary to the Law of GOD, Moses would ever have dissembled the matter. Nay, and the Scripture informs us, that David *was a man after GOD'S own heart*; and that, so long as he lived, *he was obedient to all the LORD'S Commandments;* excepting only in *Uriah's* affair. So that, had it been a sin to have diverse wives, and seeing, also, that it was a matter sufficiently known, and far from being a private practice, the writer would have excepted against it, or he must make himself a liar, by saying, that David *committed only that sin* of homicide, under which his adultery is comprehended. Then again, how could that be true, which GOD said to David, when, blaming him for his unthankfulness, He told him that He *had given him many wives*; who, doubtless, must have been all *whores,* except the first; and so it must not have been GOD, but the Devil. who gave them to him. Moreover, you will there find GOD to have made a Law; *that if any man had two wives, the one beloved, the other hated, and by them had diverse children, and of whom the eldest male was born of the hated woman, the father should not be allowed to make the son of his beloved wife his heir.* Now it might happen, that the beloved woman was the first wife, and so it might come to pass, that, although the husband had children by the latter sooner than by the former, yet, were your assertions just, they would be bastards, as being born of a whore, and consequently incapable of being heirs. By the Word of GOD it is, therefore, true, that all the children are alike legitimate, and sprung from diverse wives, by one and the same husband; and that, therefore, not only the first, but all the succeeding marriages are lawful, seeing GOD Himself did approve and bless them, in those holy men the Patriarchs, or primitive fathers of the world.

Ochy. The first consequence of my opinion is, you say, *that all who died actually possessed of a plurality of wives, must needs be damned.* To this I answer, *that,* *in case they died, not having put away all but the first wife, without repenting of that their sin, in particular, they absolutely are damned*: But such of them as are Saved, did repent of the sin, and divorce all, except the first, and only lawful wife.

Tely. But is it not apparent, that ever any did so; and yet, if your opinion were true, mention ought to be made thereof in Sacred Writ, whereby we might be given to understand, that to have a plurality of wives is a detestable abomination.

Ochy. It already was sufficiently known, that men ought not to have any more than only one wife, by reason that GOD had ordained, that the husband and wife should, of two, become one flesh.

Tely. Far is it from being likely, that it was not lawful to have several wives, and that the unlawfulness thereof was known, yet that Abraham, Jacob, David, with other worthy persons like them, should nevertheless openly marry more wives than one.

Ochy. That is really very good! As if many good, pious people, in ancient times, did not sin, although they knew what they were doing to be unlawful.

Tely. But they did not persevere in those sins to their lives' end, as did those who entertained a plurality of wives.

Ochy. I told you before, that, *if they were of GOD'S Elect, they did at last repent.*

Tely. But then, we ought not any longer to account those Patriarchs for saints, and quote them for patterns of goodness and piety, seeing we are assured of their having sinned, as you urge, by having a diversity of wives, but we have not any assurance at all of their having repented.

Ochy. True; unless the Word of GOD assures us that they were saints: As for example, we know Abraham, Isaac and Jacob to be Saints, because Christ says, that *many should come from the East, and from the West, and sit down, with Abraham, Isaac and Jacob, in the Kingdom of Heaven.* Now, I conclude, that Moses permitted the Jews, because of the hardness of their hearts, to put away their wives without just cause; so likewise, for the same reason, he suffered them to have several wives; that is to say, he did not hinder, nor forbid it, nor punish the same, by any Law enact in his commonwealth. But it does not, therefore, follow, that they did not sin in the sight of GOD; nor that they deserved not punishment, unless they repented.

Tely. Those things are all permitted, which are neither hindered, forbid, nor punished. Truly, I will not say Moses sinned, if, to avoid a greater evil, and to comport with the Jews' hardness of heart, he permitted them to have sundry wives; that is to say, *he neither hindered, nor punished them*: But, if he permitted them so as not even to forbid it them, I cannot say but that he did sin. For, Moses ought expressly to have forbidden, that any man should have more than one wife; which because he has not anywhere done, we must needs conclude, that it is not a thing unlawful.

Ochy. Plurality of wives was then, as it is now, so apparently vicious, filthy, and indecent, that it was needless for Moses to forbid it.

Tely. And was it not as apparent, that adultery was a thing vicious, filthy, and indecent? Yea, incomparably more so than diversity of wives: Yet he very expressly forbad adultery. But, in case it had been unlawful to have sundry wives, he ought to have inhibited that so much the more expressly, by how much the unlawfulness thereof was less manifest than was the unlawfulness of adultery. Is it not a clear case, that murder is unlawful? Yet he forbids that. In short; what are the Ten Commandments, but an express epitome of the Laws of Nature?

Ochy. It might be said, that GOD might remit the transgressions against the Second Table, because He is not only above all creatures, but above His own Law: And, perhaps, He might remit the same to all mankind, born before the death of Christ, and, consequently, be willing they should have a diversity of wives, without sin: And so it comes to pass, that they, under the Old Law, who had more wives than one, did not sin; and, under that consideration, GOD might give many wives to David. Although it may, likewise, be said, that He gave them to him only thus; He permitted him to have them, inasmuch as He neither hindered, nor punished him.

Tely. If your assertion be just, that the unlawfulness of entertaining more than one wife is clear from the Word of GOD, who said, that *two should be made one flesh*; yet that GOD did so far remit of His Laws, that men should not sin in having more, does not appear in GOD'S Word: That opinion of yours, therefore, has not any good foundation.

Ochy. If you will but recollect well, you will find, that Lamech, a very wicked man, was the first who had two wives. Other pious men, who preceded him, knowing the will of GOD, had only each of them one wife.

Tely. As if Abraham, Isaac and Jacob, were not holier Men than any of those you hint at! But, in the first place, I am at a loss to divine, how you came to be so positive that Lamech was the first man who had two wives; he is, indeed, the first mentioned in scripture to have had two. But as this is a vain argument; so, since the Scripture does not anywhere mention Cain's having more than one son, must it therefore be an undisputable consequence, that he had no more? Nor is the following less vain. It is not anywhere in Scripture recorded, that those men who lived before Lamech had more wives than one: Ergo, none of them had more than one wife. Moreover, where it is said, that Lamech had two wives, it is not charged on him as a sin, or crime, but seems rather to be intimated as a thing pleasing in GOD'S eye, that a man should have more wives than one; seeing, by them, He gave to Lamech such ingenious sons, who became the inventors of Arts and Sciences, not only delightful but profitable. Neither can I perceive, how you came to be informed, that Lamech was so very wicked a man as you would insinuate.

Ochy. GOD plagued him, by suffering him to fall into the sins of murder and despair, merely on account of his having married two wives.

Tely. For my part, I cannot conceive him to have been either a murderer, or that he fell into despair, nor are we taught anything like all that by the Scriptures, if they are rightly interpreted; or even had the Scripture intimated any such matter, which I do not grant, yet can it not from thence appear, that GOD suffered him so to go astray, purely for having married two wives.

Ochy. But, we may reasonably conjecture, that his having two wives was displeasing to GOD; since the said murder is mentioned presently after.

Tely. First, I have told you already, that, by the Words of that Text, if they be understood rightly, there is not any sound implication either of his homicide, or despair: And even if such were ever so plainly demonstrated, I say, it does not therefore follow, that his diversity of wives was the occasion, or that GOD was offended with him on that account; inasmuch as, immediately on the mention of his two wives, the LORD commends their sons; as if He would have us to understand, that He approves of such plurality of wives. Add to this, that nothing ought to be affirmed, or asserted, in GOD'S Church, as necessary to Salvation, if it be not otherwise to be known than barely by conjecture.

Ochy. Seeing I am not like to convince you from the Old Testament, I will try what is to be done with you from the New Law.

Tely. You err, if you judge the Old Law not to be sufficient to teach every article of what is necessary to Salvation. If therefore that be your reason for having recourse to the New Testament, you are deceived: Seeing, as St. Paul writes; *All Scripture, of Divine Inspiration, is profitable for reprehension, correction and instruction in righteousness, that the man of GOD may be made perfect, furnished for every good work.* Now, it is clear, that Paul, in that place, speaks of those Scriptures wherein Timothy had been exercised from his infancy: And, because the New Law was afterwards written, you must be forced to acknowledge, that Paul, there, speaks of the Old Testament. The Old Law, therefore, is profitable, not only to assert the truth of such things as are necessary to Salvation, but likewise to confute falsities; and, consequently to render a man perfect: For which cause, Christ, speaking thereof, says; *Search the Scriptures, for in them is found Eternal Life.*

Ochy. Perhaps, some certain things are prohibited to us, in the New Testament, which were not forbidden in the Old.

Tely. In matters of morality, whatever is unlawful, and to us prohibited, was in like manner evermore forbidden to them; and also, whatever was allowed and commanded to them, the same is likewise allowed and commanded to us. GOD was equally Author of the Old Testament and of the New; nor was He ever contrary, or unlike to Himself.

Ochy. We may say, that some things were allowed to those under the Old Law, because of their imperfection, which are not allowed to us, in whom carnalities should be abundantly more curbed and mortified.

Tely. You take for granted what you have not proved; *viz.* That it is unlawful to have more than one wife. Nay again, you are in the wrong, if you hold it to be bad to have one wife, but worse to have two: For as the matrimonial act, in him who has one wife, is a thing not in itself evil, nor repugnant to those actions which are necessary to Salvation, no more is it evil to have two, or more wives, provided a man has a call from above to marry them, and is moved, not merely by the impulse of the flesh, but of the spirit, that he may have children, and bring them up in the fear of GOD; his wives also doing the same. Whence it follows, that he who has two, or more wives, may be as perfect as he who has but one, or none. Nor had Abraham, because he had sundry wives, a scantier portion of faith, hope, or charity than priests, monks, or friars, who marry not at all. Conjugal chastity is as well the Gift of GOD as is that of celibacy. For this cause, St. Paul said; *Everyone is endowed with his Gift from GOD, some one way, some another.* 2 Corinthians 7.

Ochy. In that place, the Apostle exhorted the Corinthians to a single life; and that for no other reason, than because a married state has many encumbrances attending it: Inasmuch as married people, being entangled with worldly affairs, are not so free to pray and preach up and down, and do good to others, as are those who are single. Now, if the having one wife brings along with it so many impediments, one may readily conjecture, what a plurality of wives will do. Ergo, to have more than one, is absolutely unlawful.

Tely. You are in an error, if you imagine, that St. Paul's meaning, in those words, was, that marriage impeded men in their journey heavenwards, so that married people could not be Saved: For then what GOD said would not be true; *viz.* That *it was not good for a man to be alone.* But it would rather be most meritoriously excellent to be alone, and to marry at all, would be the vilest deed one could do, as being a mortal sin. So far from that, I cannot but hold, that a married man may not only be Saved as well as a single one, but also be as completely perfect as he; inasmuch as he may attain to as great perfection, in faith, hope, and charity, as the other: And if he cannot personally perform some external works, which the bachelor can, as impeded by his matrimonial encumbrances, yet he may perform the same in heart and mind; which is what GOD most regards.

Ochy. Though matrimony itself does not deprive a man of a future felicity, yet his having more wives than one, does.

Tely. How prove you that?

Ochy. From Paul; who, speaking of bishops, says; He would have them be the *husbands of one wife*: Meaning, that they should not have more. It is therefore unlawful to have more wives than one.

Tely. Nay; rather when he tells them, expressly by naming the office, that one wife they should have, lest, having more, they should be too much encumbered with mundane affairs, it is easy to comprehend, that he allowed other men to have more.

Ochy. St. Paul's mind is, by some, interpreted, *A bishop is to have but one wife;* that is, say they, *the Church for his Spiritual Spouse.*

Tely. Many reasons demonstrate this to be a very false opinion. First; because Christ only is the Spouse of souls, and Bridegroom of His Church: And if we, who are ministers, be His friends, we ought, with John the Baptist, as the friends of Christ, the only true Spouse of souls, to send them to Him, their Bridegroom; and not to draw them to ourselves. Christ's churches, therefore, are not the bishops' spouses: And if they were, as a husband is his wife's superior, so should they be to their respective churches; against which writes Paul to the Corinthians, where his words are; *We are not lords over your faith, or over you by reason of your faith.* The Church, therefore, is not Paul's wife. I confess, indeed, that one church is sufficient for one pastor; and he merits no small praise, if he can govern that as it ought to be governed. In the ancient times of Christianity; one church had sometimes diverse pastors, as appears from the Epistle to the Philippians, in which Paul salutes the bishops who were at Philippi: Whereas nowadays, one bishop has many churches. Also, when

Paul says; *A bishop ought to have one wife*: he speaks of the manners of him who was fit to be a bishop: But in case he be yet to be chosen, he is no bishop; and therefore, as yet, has no church which may be called his wife. From hence, likewise, it is manifest, that, by wife, he did not mean church; because, almost presently after those words, he makes mention of his children, ordaining, that *he govern well his family, and keep his children in subjection to him, with all due reverence.* For if a man cannot govern his own family, how can he preside over GOD'S Church? Wherefore, in that place, he assuredly speaks of a wife, and not of a church.

Ochy. Some affirm, that Paul, there, forbids such men to be chosen bishops as have had more than one wife, though not at one time.

Tely. Yet I cannot conceive, that Paul deemed it a sin for a man, after the decease of his first wife, to take to him a second; forasmuch as he himself says; That *after the husband's death, the wife is free, and may, without blame, marry another.* So far is it from being unlawful for a man, after the death of one wife, to espouse another.

Ochy. It is held to be a very enormous shame, for a man to marry again when his first wife is dead.

Tely. If you rightly weigh the matter, and follow not the opinions of the blind, senseless vulgar, you will find the matrimonial act to be as free from any turpitude, as the acts of eating and drinking: Nor would GOD have enjoined matrimony, had it been evil; which, nevertheless, He expressly did, when He said, *Increase and Multiply.*

Ochy. I condemn not matrimony; but the iteration, or repetition thereof.

Tely. The second nuptials are as true and valid as the first: And therefore you cannot condemn the iteration of matrimony, without condemning also matrimony itself. Take one instance. A young man marries a wife; she dies a few days after; he is naturally incontinent, or has a second call to the matrimonial state: In this case, who is ignorant, that, answerably to the very precept of Paul, since he cannot contain, he may and ought to take another wife?

Ochy. Were not second marriages filthy and unlawful, Paul would not, speaking afterwards of widows, have commanded such to be chosen as had not more than one husband.

Tely. Conceive you Paul to have been a person inclined to superstition?
Ochy. I do not conceive him to have been such.
Tely. Had a sprightly young widow, somewhat incontinent, applied herself to Paul, for his advice; what think you his answer would have been?
Ochy. That *she should remarry*; according to his doctrine and precept.
Tely. Repeated marriages are not, therefore, unlawful. Why, then, should Paul reject such widows as had been married oftener than once? For it was very possible, that some widows, having had diverse husbands, might be infinitely chaster, and more pious than those who had wedded only one. It might also happen, that she who had several husbands, might have lived with them only one year; whereas she who had one only husband, might have cohabited with him thirty or forty years: And in such case, I cannot really see, why *this* should be worthier to be chosen, than *that*. My belief, therefore, is, that Paul's mind, in that place, was this; That *such widows were not to be chosen as had been divorced from several husbands, and had married in the lifetimes of those husbands from whom they were divorced*: For they were either divorced on just grounds,

and it was not fit they should be chosen, or on unjust grounds, and so the marriage remained good, having never been violated, and the divorced woman had committed a sin if she married another: Hence it was, that all divorced women were counted infamous, not only such as married again to others, but, likewise, such as abstained from wedlock, especially among the Gentiles who used not to divorce their wives, except for some fault, or vicious quality. Paul, therefore, did not ever condemn those women who remarried after the decease of a former husband; neither did he prohibit those men to be bishops, who married another woman when their former wife was dead; which, nevertheless, the superstitious papists observe, because they understand not Paul's meaning. Among them, though a man has entertained ever so many strumpets, they make him a bishop; but, his first wife being dead, if he marry another, they absolutely will not: Whence it comes to pass, that matrimony with them, is of a worse report, and far more scandalous, than either fornication, adultery, incest, sacrilege, sodomy, or any other of the most execrable abominations one can imagine. Paul's mind (as has been observed concerning widows, and this will make the third opinion) is, That *he who has had diverse wives, by reason he divorced one, ought not to be made a bishop: For if he divorced her unjustly, he ought not to be made a bishop, in that regard; if justly, yet his wife's infamy, redounding on himself, does that way incapacitate him*; And on this account it was, that Paul would not agree he should be a bishop. Nevertheless, I cannot favor these sentiments: For, he says not; he must *have been*; but says; he must *be* the husband of one wife; for he says; he must be blameless, *viz.* as the husband of one wife; as he expresses it, a little after, with relation to deacons, and writing to Titus concerning bishops.

Ochy. By reason that bishops, in regard of the public office they bear, as also deacons, have dealings with all sorts of persons, not only men but women, Paul, to avoid suspicion, would have them to be married: And this, perhaps, might be the meaning of those words. It may, likewise, possibly be that the Apostle, foreseeing the future papistical superstition prohibiting the marriage of bishops, etc., that they might be without excuse, said; *They ought to be blameless, and to have a wife*: But, indeed, he did not expressly say, *they are to have one only, and no more*. Or he shows, that a Bishop should have a wife, that is, he should be satisfied with her, and not to have any kind of unclean dealings with other women: All which is no other than enjoining him to be chaste and honest.

Tely. Paul's mind here is, certainly, neither more nor less than thus: That *it is lawful for the generality of Christians to have a plurality of wives; but for each bishop to have no more than one*: Not that it was sinful for them to have more; but because the duty of bishops being to labor for the Salvation of others, he was apprehensive lest a multiplicity of wives might be a remora, or obstacle to the due performance of their function. On this account, he would not admit their having more than one; nor is it, therefore, unlawful for other men to have more: Nay, while he forbids bishops and deacons, by name, to have a plurality of wives, he tacitly allows it to others. Nor is it at all likely, that Paul would have prohibited bishops having more than one wife, had it not been then usual for them to have more. It was, therefore, in the New Testament forbidden to bishops to have a plurality of wives, as, in the Old Testament it was forbidden to kings in Deuteronomy 17, not because it was in itself unlawful, but lest kings, whose office was of the greatest consequence, being distracted by their wives should become corrupt; as it happened to Solomon: For if Adam, when he had but one, was, notwithstanding, perverted by her, it is easy to conjecture what might happen to kings, if they had many. Nevertheless, I cannot but believe, that as, in the same place, he forbad kings to have many horses, meaning, a too enormous multitude of them; lest in them, rather than in GOD, they should put their trust: For otherwise, the having many horses was not disallowed. Even so, they were not forbid to have many wives; since David, a most holy man, even one after GOD'S own heart, had several; but that they should not entertain any immoderate multitude of wives, more particularly of such as were professed heathens, worshipping false deities. But to return more closely to our point: It is not credible, that Paul was apprehensive of Timothy's electing for bishops such as were unbaptized Jews or Gentiles: It is, therefore, plain, that, in Christ's church, among the primitive Christians, there were men who had more wives than one; and because from among them a bishop was to be chosen, he was against his making choice of a person who had a plurality of wives. But if to entertain more wives than one had been, as you affirm it to be, repugnant to GOD'S

Law, and the first wife only being rightful and legal, and the others all harlots, it is not in the least credible, that the Christian pastors would have administered baptism to any man who had a plurality of wives, unless he put away all except his first: And had that been the practice, it would have been very needless in Paul to ordain, that he who was to be chosen bishop should be the husband of one only wife; since the whole community of Christians, from among whom he was to be elected, had each of them no more than one. But what I much marvel at, is, that many, who not only firmly believe, but maintain in their writings, That *it is utterly contrary to Law, both Moral and Natural to have more than one wife,* do yet, in expounding Paul, affirm, that, writing to Timothy, *he cautions him not to choose for a bishop one who had a plurality of wives*; whence necessarily it follows, that, since election was not to be made of any who was not within the pale of Christ's Church, the Church of Christ had within it such as had more wives than one, and consequently did not think it unlawful to have more: Otherwise, had the Christians counted it unlawful, as they did not baptize, or admit unto the Lord's Supper, any man who entertained a concubine, except he would forsake her, so they would not have baptized, nor admitted to the Lord's Supper, nor even have suffered among them, such as had a diversity of wives, except they would divorce all but the first.

Ochy. But what reply can you make to Paul's willing and commanding; That *every man should have his own wife*? For in saying, *his own wife,* he certainly excludes *wives*.

Tely. According to some, his meaning is; *Let every man have his own wife:* That is, *his own,* not another man's; and not, *one only*: As if a father, pointing towards a daughter of his, should say; *This is my* own *daughter*; yet still not gainsaying, that he has other daughters, which are also his *own*.

Ochy. Paul does likewise, in the same place, ordain; That *each wife shall have her own proper husband*; meaning such a wife as is peculiar and proper to him alone, and not in common with other wives: And hence it certainly follows, that as a wife ought to be proper and peculiar to her husband, and not to appertain to other husbands, so the husband ought to be appropriated to his first wife, and not common to others, if you design (as you should do) so to expound Paul's text that he may not contradict himself.

Tely. Paul does not there dispute, a man's having, or not having, a plurality of wives; but his intent is to show, that those men who have not the Gift of Continence, should take to them wives; and that women under the same circumstances should marry.

Ochy. Can you, possibly, not comprehend, that a plurality of wives is repugnant to the matrimonial contract, in which both man and woman reciprocally yield up to each other, during life, the honest use of their respective bodies? On which account, also, Paul says; that *neither of them have power over their own bodies, but each over the other's respectively*: And a man having once granted the honest use of his body to his wife, he may not afterwards give the same to any other, he having already given it up to the first, who is become the rightful owner thereof.

Tely. Yes, with the consent of the first he may; as did Abraham, when, by Sarah's permission, he went in unto Hagar; and consequently, with the consent of his first and second, a man may marry a third; which is as right in other men as in Abraham; especially where the wives are given to understand, that it is not sinful for their husbands, with their permission, to take to them other wives.

Ochy. Believe you, that David, when he espoused Bathsheba, had the consent of his other wives so to do, and that others who took to them a diversity of wives, did it with their former wives' approbation?

Tely. Supposing they had it not; nevertheless their marriages were as true and lawful as if otherwise: It being then a matter universally known, and by multitudes of examples confirmed, that it was not in any way unlawful for a man to have several wives: so that when, by matrimony, a man granted to his wife the use of his body, he gave it not up to her so entirely as utterly to bereave himself of all power to participate the same to other wives; to all which the wives, by the public custom then in force, were no strangers, and tacitly acquiesced to it, since they knew their husbands took them on those conditions understood: Their marriages, therefore, were lawful and valid.

Ochy. No man can marry a second wife without wronging his first: Nor is it credible, that wives did ever cordially consent to their husbands doing them such manifest injury as to marry others.

Tely. Possibly my wife may prove barren; in which case, it is absolutely her duty to consent I take another; nay, of her own accord, to advise me so to do, as did Sarah: And should she disapprove thereof, she would therein do unjustly, and so her husband may most legally espouse another woman, in spite of her unjust opposition. Likewise, when a wife is pregnant, and for some time after her delivery, since she is then unfit for her husband's society, and also when she is dire tempered or aged, her husband, without any wrong done to her, may have dealings with another wife: Nay, though a wife has no ailing at all, and is apt for procreation, yet ought she to be satisfied with having, at certain meet times, the enjoyment of her husband's society, and to leave him at free liberty to distribute the rest of his conversation, as he sees proper, among his other wives.

Ochy. May a woman lawfully, think you, have a plurality of husbands?

Tely. Certainly, no.

Ochy. Yet are there infirm men, as well as there are ailing and distempered women, Likewise can a woman admit of dealings with more men, than a man is able to have with women: Wherefore it is seemingly more just, or at least less unjust, that a woman should have a plurality of husbands, than that a man should have several wives.

Tely. Nay, nay; rather, seeing that matrimony was ordained chiefly for procreation-sake, and a man having a diversity of wives may, in a short space of time, have abundance more children than can a woman with diverse husbands, it is undoubtedly more equitable for a man to have many wives, than for a woman to have more than one husband. But the principal reasons why women ought not, by any means, to be allowed a diversity of husbands, and yet men may have diverse wives, are these: One, and the main reason of all, is that, by women's having a diversity of husbands, the world would be nothing but disorder, dissention and confusion; since, as no husband could know, with any the least certainty, the offspring his wife brings to be his own, he might always suspect them to be another man's, and of consequence, would not take such care of their education and welfare, as husbands now do, and with some reason, as presuming them to be his, though born of diverse wives; nay, very likely, being so unassured of their being his own children, he would not appoint them to be his heirs. Another reason why it is legal for men to have several wives, but not for women to have a diversity of husbands, is this: A husband is his wife's head, and has over her command and authority, as being her superior; for which cause he may have many wives, if he is in a capacity of managing, instructing, and entertaining them as he ought: Nor is it in any way monstrous, but rather very comely, to have several members to a body, though but one head; but a body which has more than one head, is a monster: So for one husband to have diverse wives, is not at all monstrous; but for one wife to have a diversity of husbands, is most monstrous. Wherefore, as there, unavoidably, would be discord and confusion for one body to have more than one head, and those heads dissent in opinion, as might well be; so would there be horrible dissentions, feuds and inconveniences, if wives had a diversity of husbands; since the husbands might have contrary minds, and lay on their wives injunctions quite different one from the other.

Ochy. If we regard discords and inconveniencies, we shall find them sometimes to have been excessive, on account of a man's having two wives; as appears by the stories of Sarah and Hagar, Leah and Rachel, Hannah and Peninnah, and several others among whom reigned perpetual Dissentions: The which, possibly, the ALMIGHTY did permit, as a token of his displeasure at men's having a plurality of wives.

Tely. Though between the firstborn and their brethren, grievous quarrels and hatred have frequently arisen, as in Cain and Abel, in Esau and Jacob, with innumerable more, it is not therefore displeasing in GOD'S sight, that men should have a numerous progeny: And likewise, though there is seldom much amity and peace between mothers-in-law and their daughters-in-law, yet matrimony is not displeasing to GOD. So, in like manner, though among diverse wives of the same husband there has seldom been good agreement, yet cannot either matrimony itself in general, or the marriage of sundry wives to one man, be therefore justly condemned, but only such wives as had not dispositions so good as they should have had.

Ochy. Christians, in this life, ought to be condemners of pleasures, and to have more of the Spirit than those who had lived under the Old Law. Wherefore, notwithstanding those our predecessors had a plurality of wives, we ought certainly to be satisfied with each of us one.

Tely. It is needless I repeat it, having already declared to you my sentiment, that it is far from being unlawful for a man to cohabit with a diversity of wives; neither is it in any way inconsistent with the most elevated degree of faith and perfection. Nor can I comprehend from whence you can be assured, that some Christians have not a call from the ALMIGHTY to cohabit with sundry wives, as well as some of the Jews were, by Him, heretofore called so to do.

Ochy. Urge whatever you can, to have a plurality of wives is both dishonest, indecent and filthy.

Tely. You are dragged into this erroneous opinion, by two things. The first is custom: For if it were customary for men to have more wives than one, you would not look on it to be either blamable or unseemly. The other is a certain hypocritical sanctity, which induces you to fancy the having more than one wife to be a thing unlawful, though it is not at all repugnant to Sacred Writ: And such as are convicted of having more wives than one, have far greater punishments inflicted on them than would be, should they entertain a thousand harlots.

Ochy. A man finds it no easy matter to satisfy one woman; yet you would have it allowable for him to have a plurality!

Tely. A Husband is not bound to satiate all his wife's carnal appetites, but only such as are moderated with reason.

Ochy. Under the Old Testament, when the world was but thinly peopled, it was, perhaps, fitting, that men should have a plurality of wives: But now that the earth is so very populous as it is, there is no manner of necessity for it.

Tely. In answer to that; first, you are not certain, whether men, in case they had a diversity of wives, would be much more fruitful in children than they are: Or even if their offspring (as probably it might) should prove abundantly more numerous, how know you but that the products of the earth would be so increased as to afford a sufficiency for their nourishment, and all their other necessities? For the same GOD, who had so multiplied mankind, might also increase and multiply the fruits to a competent plenty for their sustenance. But, suppose you were certain, that they would all perish from poverty, yet of so high price are the souls of men, that we ought not, by any means, to prevent their existence, especially if we are thereunto called by our Creator, as were, of old, those holy men who had a plurality of wives.

Ochy. In these days of ours, a Christian should not have more than one wife; if for no other reason, than at least to avoid the scandal and offence the which would thence arise; since all Christians look on the having more wives than one to be a thing not only most detestably filthy, but even diabolical.

Tely. Just so, as even though the generality of men should combine to account matrimony itself to be utterly unlawful and abominable, yet ought you not regard the offence it gives them, but marry, if you had thereunto a call; so ought you also to marry more than one, if you were thereunto stimulated by Divine impulse.

Ochy. A single man, indeed, in such a case might marry, to avoid falling into uncleanness, though some may take offence at his so doing; especially if he had a call to it from above. But he who already has one wife, has no need to take another; neither will he be thereunto called by impulse Divine.

Tely. Nay certainly, if his wife be infirm, or troubled with any other impediment, so that he cannot have due enjoyment of her, and he has not the Gift of Continence, he necessarily must, to avoid uncleanness, marry another. Add to this, that it is not merely to avoid uncleanness that GOD calls men to marry, but chiefly for procreation sake, as of old He called Abraham, and other holy men.

Ochy. Shall I make it clearly manifest to you, that the having more than one wife is a thing actually prohibited? Christ says; That *if any man puts away his wife, except for adultery, and shall marry another, he commits adultery.* But if a man might have more wives than one, would he not commit adultery, for Christ says, whether he puts away his former wife, or no.

Tely. No man can better expound those words of Christ, than Christ himself; Who, in another place, explaining the last words, says; *Whoever shall put away his wife, except for adultery, causes her to commit adultery.* That is to say; he gives occasion to his wife, so unjustly put away, to commit adultery: For the wife being thus deprived of her rightful husband, cannot, during his life, espouse any other without being guilty of adultery. Therefore Christ says not; *If any man puts away his wife, not for adultery, and marries another, he commits adultery;* but that, *he gives his repudiated wife occasion to commit adultery.*

Ochy. Matthew, Mark and Luke all record, that Christ said; *If any man puts away his wife, and marries another, he commits adultery;*

meaning, by marrying that other. But if His meaning was to show, that, by his divorcing her unjustly, he gave her occasion to commit adultery, it would have been sufficient to have said; *If any man puts away his wife, he commits adultery;* without adding, *and marries another.* Wherefore Christ, by those His Words, in Matthew 5, designed not to expound that expression in chapter 19 of the said evangelist, where He only said; *If any man puts away his wife, not for adultery, he makes her commit adultery.* But, elsewhere, he expresses Himself differently; *Viz.* That *if he marries another, in the same way, he commits adultery:* Because the first only was his wife, and it was not lawful he should have more than one. To this add, that Christ's Words, in his Sermon upon the Mount, were spoken before those were uttered, by which He answered the Pharisees, who asked him; *Whether a man, for every cause, might put away his wife?* Wherefore those Words cannot be the exposition of these, which were spoken afterwards.

Tely. Whether the latter Words were an exposition of the former, or not, I am satisfied, that both mean one and the same thing; *Viz.* That *if any man shall put away his wife, without just cause, he* *occasions her to commit adultery*: And as for the additional Words, in Chapter 19, Christ added them only to demonstrate, that if a wife, unjustly divorced, marries another man, she commits adultery; though, at the same time, her former husband has married another woman; Since her first matrimony is not void, by her husband's remarriage, but continues in its full force. Christ's meaning, is, therefore, this: *If he puts her away without just cause, though he marries another, yet he gives to her, who is so put away, occasion to commit adultery.*

Ochy. You so force and strain this your interpretation, that it is in the greatest danger of breaking. Nay, we may also see even irrational creatures, that each male has its peculiar female, with which alone it couples, as in birds of all kinds: And much more does it become men, particularly Christians, to do the like.

Tely. This is fact only in such creatures whose propagation is not of much necessity towards man's sustenance: But, by observation, you may find one cock to have many hens; one bull many cows;

Note: A man who takes an unbetrothed virgin as a wife, whether the man so doing be married or not, cannot commit adultery with her, for she is not another man's wife.

Leviticus 20:10 10 And the man that commits adultery *with another man's wife,* namely *he that commits adultery with his neighbor's wife*, the adulterer and the adulteress shall surely be put to death.

and the same in many other creatures of utility to mankind. If, therefore, by Divine Ordinance, and for man's benefit, one cock has many hens, much more is it the ALMIGHTY'S pleasure, that a man may have several women, for the propagation of men, whom he so tenderly loves and so highly prizes.

Ochy. Were none of those creatures, you mention, emasculated by castration, and were assembled together in great numbers, you would find each male with only his own peculiar female; much more ought it to be so with men: But, very many of the males being castrated, and few of the species together in one place, if one male does couple with diverse females, it does not, therefore, follow, that one man should have diverse wives. Into the Ark of Noah the ALMIGHTY sent just as many males as females, to show, that each male should have only his own single female.

Tely. I confess, that were the number of men and women in the world exactly equal, it would be very desirable, that each man should have only a single wife. But since the number of women is far greater, I conceive it to be reasonable for one man to have diverse women; for it is not in vain that GOD creates a greater number of females, of our species, than

He does males. But, suppose, for example, there were, in the whole world, only 300 women, and just as many men, and every man had one woman; they would, after a time, propagate their kind as if 400 of the 600 were females, and 200 males, each of which had two women. And on this account it is, that GOD is pleased to create more women than men: The life of one man being equal to those of two women.

Ochy. Hold! In the first place, I believe not, that you can be certain of there being more women in the world than there are men. You, perhaps, fancy so, because we are apt to rejoice at the birth of a boy, and the contrary for a girl. And even admit, that more girls are born into the world than boys, yet the majority of them are very short-lived, by reason of their tenderer constitution. Besides, abundance more men than women are destroyed by war, shipwreck, the sword of justice, etc. Yet none of this can be a sufficient plea for, or proof of the necessity or legality of polygamy. And as for the love of carnal society, it is a passion than which no passion is more violent: And if even a dishonest love cannot brook a partnership, much less should that which is honest and irreproachable!

Note: Christian churches currently average more than two women members for every one man member and Christians are forbidden from marrying outside their faith so the situation that Tely describes is true for the churches.

Tely. Pious love rather extends to all mankind, even to our very enemies.

Ochy. Jacob was a pious, good man; and yet he loved barren Rachel more than fruitful Leah: So also did Elkanah love barren Hannah better than he did Peninnah, who was otherwise. Solomon likewise said, that his beloved was one. Wherefore it is a very difficult task for a man to distribute his affection and benevolence, equally and impartially, among several wives, which, yet, must be done where polygamy is admitted. When a man has but one wife, a reciprocal love is better preserved than if he had a plurality; and in case of any quarrel between a man and his single wife, they are more easily reconciled. Amidst a plurality of wives, contrary opinions abound, and there never lacks a comfortless scene of discord and distraction.

The fault lies not in polygamy, but in the fractious dispositions of those discording females!

Tely

Tely. Were there a call from GOD, their state would not be without the Divine benediction. Polygamy is no enemy to concord and charity. Therefore if a man has several wives, and there is no agreement among them, the fault lies not in polygamy, but in the fractious dispositions of those discording females.

Ochy. If the filthy love of a vile strumpet is, often, the occasion of a man's being satisfied with her only, abundantly more should a like effect be worked by the sacred love of matrimony.

Tely. We daily see, that some filthy love has a better effect on some, than the sacred matrimonial love has on others; also, in like manner, superstition produces more good in some, than does True Religion in others; all which is owing to the instigation and influence of the Devil.

Ochy. That polygamy is repugnant to Natural Reason is manifest in its being ever abstained from by all nations, as a thing not lawful.

Tely. You are sensible, that the light of nature, I mean, that Natural Law which men have in their hearts imprinted, is the Gift of GOD, and that it is just, and that the Law of Moses is not contrary to it, but an explanation thereof: For if the Law of Moses were repugnant to the Law of Nature,

GOD would be contrary to Himself, since they both proceed from GOD, or rather both are one and the same Law. Wherefore, if plurality of wives had been repugnant to Reason, certainly, neither would Moses have indulged it, those holy good Patriarchs have practiced it, nor the ALMIGHTY have suffered it. When GOD, by Moses, commanded the Israelites, that when they came upon the borders of the Gentiles, they should not imitate their vices, He would, among other prohibited practices, have named polygamy, had it been contrary to Law; and He would, by Moses, have forbid it, which He did not: Neither do we anywhere read, that GOD ever punished any man for his having a plurality of wives, nor that by his prophets, they were even once threatened, on that account. If you desire to make the manners of the Gentiles your Rule and Law, you will find them abounding in wickedness. And as to your assertion, that all nations abstained from and abhorred polygamy, it is a falsity, as appears in the Hebrews: Also Chremes had two wives, if we may credit Terence; so had Boocus, as we are told by Sallust: And to conclude, so had Socrates himself, who, nevertheless, was a most wise man, and had a very plentiful portion of the light of Nature.

Ochy. Even the wisest of men sometimes err.

Tely. None did ever condemn, or reprehend Socrates, on account of his bigamy, or having two wives, though he has been much censured on other accounts. But why should we use multiplicity of arguments? Polygamy was, and still is, practiced as a beneficial custom, most profitable to mankind by advancing propagation, not only among the Jews, but likewise by the Persians, Turks, and others. In Europe only it is deemed abominable; in which Europe, vice has abounded, and still does, if not more, yet not one jot less, than in any other part of the universe. Nay, in former ages, polygamy has been favorably looked on even in Europe; only they avoided having, in one house, more than one mistress of the family, which was a piece of prudence, as being very convenient to prevent noise and confusion.

Ochy. Well, but what say you to the Imperial Laws, which make quite against you?

Tely. Whereabouts, pray, is that?

Ochy. First of all, the Emperors Dioclesianus and Maximinus, absolutely prohibit polygamy, in these words: That *no man, within the jurisdiction of the Roman Empire,* *can have two wives*: Since, also, in the Praetorian Edict, such men are branded with *infamy*; which delinquency no equitable judge will suffer to pass with impunity. The same code likewise says: *undoubtedly, the man who has two wives, is not free from infamy.*

Tely. You say, the authors of the first Imperial Law were Dioclesianus and Maximinus: The other is taken from a rescript of the Emperors Valerianus and Galienus.

Ochy. It suffices, that being emperors, they were invested with the power of enacting laws.

Tely. We must not forget, that, in the Pagan Empire, such was the matrimonial constitution, that, for any light and frivolous cause, men might turn out their wives, and entertain harlots at discretion, without much reproach: Yet such concubines had neither the name nor the authority of wives. On this account the emperors made those decrees, not because they deemed polygamy to be unlawful, seeing they allowed a plurality of legal concubines; but they judged it reasonable, that the first alone should bear the title and privileges of a wife; more particularly, since the man might part with her if she suited him not.

Ochy. But we see, that the Emperor Constantinus prohibited all concubinage.

Tely. If you weigh well his words, you will comprehend, that his intention was only to inhibit him who had a wife to entertain concubines; not that the having them was actually illegal, but a man was not to have them with him in the house where his wife was; and this merely to prevent contention and disquiet: But separately, every man might have as many as he pleased. And the Emperor Valentinianus, invested with a like power and authority, did not only permit such as had wives to keep concubines, but many wives also at the same time, and in the same house, all dignified with the same title, and bearing equal authority: The said emperor himself, also had a diversity of wives. Now this Law of Valentinianus, which was of a later date than that of Constantinus, did entirely abrogate the same, so that it became void.

Ochy. Justinianus makes not any mention, in his code, of this Law of Valentinianus.

Tely. Nevertheless, it undoubtedly was publicly recorded, as we are informed in history. To this we may add, that, besides, this emperor, it is well known, that Constantius, the son of Constantinus, had sundry wives. Likewise Clotarius, King of France, and Heribertus and Hypericus, his sons, had a diversity of wives. I add also, Pipinus and Carolus Magnus, of whom Urspergensis witnesses, that they had each more than one wife: Nay, we may, likewise, add Arnulphus and Fredericus Barbarossa, both Emperors of Germany, with Philippus Deodatus, King of France, and innumerable others. Not that I will deny, but that it is abominably criminal in those who, abandoning their wives, go into foreign countries, and there marry others: I only speak in behalf of those well disposed men who supposing the ALMIGHTY calls them to a diversity of wives, are mindful to maintain and cherish them all, as they ought to do.

Ochy. You are supposing what never yet was in the Creation, which is, that GOD ever called a man to a diversity of wives.

Tely. Certainly, Abraham, Jacob, and an infinity of others, were thereunto called by the LORD; and, doubtless, the like may be with us. Nor can I see, what more need had they of such a call than we have; or why it was more their duty than ours, to raise a numerous progeny.

Ochy. The Emperor Constantinus would not allow a plurality of wives, nor will the present reigning emperor.

Tely. My inquiry is after what is equitable and fitting, and not after what men in power will, or will not. Nature's Laws are immutable: And if, in Abraham's time, it was consonant to reason to have a diversity of wives, and deemed a matter neither dishonest nor unjust (for if it had, we may be assured, that good Patriarch would not have taken to his bed more than one) we must confess it to be, now, in our days, likewise just, honest and desirable; and so it was in the days of Constantinus: For, notwithstanding his imperial authority, he could not make that to be indecent and unjust, which in itself was just and honorable. Undoubtedly, that ancient Church of Christ had the knowledge of Divine matters; and yet, neither that Church, nor the emperors of those times, did condemn or punish polygamy. But in every age, men had rather seem to be good, than be so indeed; seeing they so furiously cry down a diversity of wives, yet are such lovers of adultery and fornication. Finally, to condemn polygamy, is for man to prefer himself to GOD, Who never did condemn it, and to assume a greater degree of perfection than He. I spare saying, that I may not allow of the Laws of the Emperors, in matrimonial cases; seeing they refer those matters to the Ecclesiastical Laws.

Ochy. If by them you will be tried, I am victor.

Tely. Produce me one canon which makes for you.

Ochy. In the times of the fathers of the church, polygamy was accounted so notoriously filthy and abominable, that they did not think it fitting to condemn it expressly by words.

Tely. Now I, for my part, am verily persuaded, that those fathers of the ancient church were contented with the canon of St. Paul, who would have those who were ministers of the church to be satisfied with one wife; not on account of its being in itself illegal to have more, but that they might the better attend and execute their function: But, as for all others, he allowed them to do, in that case, according to the inward motions they had from above.

Ochy. We know that, in the third and seventh Neocaesarian Councils, polygamy was prohibited.

Tely. I assert, that it never was prohibited, neither in those councils, nor in any other.

Ochy. Certain I am, that they ordained a penalty for polygamists; which never would have been done, had they not judged it illegal for a man to have more than one wife: Nay, they forbad all priests to be present at the marriages of those who would have more wives than one.

Tely. Right; they did so: But at the same time, they did not forbid polygamy itself.

Ochy. They sufficiently forbad it, when they ordained punishments for it.

Tely. Should you read through every one of the councils, you will not therein find polygamy to be prohibited. Neither can it be alleged as the reason, that they conceived it to be forbid in Scripture: Since I have already demonstrated its not being there inhibited. And, in Canon 17 of the Apostles, it is decreed; That *a man, having two wives, should be removed from the Episcopal and priestly function, and from all other ecclesiastical offices*. But had the authors of those canons looked upon polygamy itself to have been repugnant to Scripture, Christian charity, and the common good of mankind, they, assuredly, would have excommunicated all those who had more than one wife; nor would they only have banished such men from their communion, but would, likewise, have inflicted on them grievous corporal punishments. But those apostolical fathers, as Paul had done before them, forbad only the ministers of the church to have more wives than one; not as if it was a thing contrary to Christian and moral honesty, but because it would draw away and divert them from spiritual exercises. But because, in process of time, men began, by degrees, to turn aside from the right Way, so that many fell to account even matrimony itself to be unlawful; they blushed not to give it under their hands, That *a man's first wife being, dead, it was adultery, and not marriage, to take another*: Touching which matters, you may see much in Gratianus. So do, likewise, Hieronimus and Tertullianus interpret that saying of Paul and the Apostles, as if the meaning and intention was; That *he who had two wives, though successively, might not be admitted a minister of Christ's Church; neither he who espoused a widow, or a divorced wife*: All which we know to be still in force among many. And, among the Reverend of the Romish Creed, we see, that matrimony, in any sort or degree, is utterly thrown out of doors; though we daily see persons, *most Sir Reverendly noted for filthiness*, promoted to their chiefest church dignities! But mark what I am about to advance. The life of a courtier, and a soldier, cannot be deemed really sinful *in terminis*, but many may be thereunto called by GOD Himself: Yet, in the 12th Canon of the Nicene Council, it was decreed; That *those who having once quitted the profession of arms, and again went to the wars should be severely punished*; though, in those days, seldom any war was moved, except against infidels and idolaters. In like manner, had they decreed penalties for such as had two wives, bigamy does not therefore become sinful, for many be thereunto called by instinct Divine. There are abundance of such canons, particularly touching matrimony, which want amendment; not that we are tied by any canon, but such only as have their foundations on the Word of GOD. The fathers have many times erred, as being men, and not infrequently swerving from the rule of GOD'S Word. Moreover, we ought to believe, that Paul taught (for example) the Ephesians, and the rest of the churches, all things necessary to Salvation; as himself testifies: And yet he taught them not, that any were to be tied to one wife, excepting ministers of the church.

Ochy. That he might, perhaps, do, to the intent that, by their example, others might, by little and little, be brought to a like laudable practice.

Tely. In the first place, what you urge is not grounded on any part of GOD'S injunctions; without which, according to my sentiments, it is no less than impiety to force or bind consciences. Nor ought every thing which is desirable for a bishop, to be propounded as a model for all others to copy after.

Ochy. Yet, it is a bold word for us to say, that the Church has erred, now, for upwards of twelve hundred years, in condemning and punishing bigamy.

Tely. That error is not to be attributed to GOD'S Church, but to men; who, in the Church, have as much erred in prohibiting marriage to priests: Yea, and I would have you take notice, that the Neocaesarian Council did not decree, *the second wife should be divorced;* nor that *the second was no true marriage.*

Ochy. The Council sufficiently declared that, by decreeing penalties for such as had two wives.

Tely. Augustinus judges that man *to be guilty of sin, who marries, after having made a vow of chastity*: And yet he accounts such to be a *true marriage,* and that the same *ought not to be made void.* This argument is not, therefore, of any force or validity, that: *The Council enacted penalties for such as had two wives; and therefore the second was not a true marriage.* Moreover, though more than a thousand years are passed since penalties were enacted for those who had two wives, yet it is not above four hundred years since that decree was first received by the Italians, Spaniards, and Germans. And as for the institution, it is merely human; and the bishops would have exclaimed against the Emperor Valentinianus, for his plurality of wives, but that he had Scripture on his side: And, notwithstanding they reprehended such as had more than one wife, as Augustinus and Bonifacius did, as persons who seemed overindulgent to the flesh, yet they did not, therefore, excommunicate them, or deem them among the number of such as could not be Saved. Ambrosius was a very sharp reprover of sin; yet we do not anywhere read, that he reproved Valentinianus for having a diversity of wives: Yea, and the said Ambrosius, reprehending his second wife, Justina, for her Arianism, ought withal to have reprehended her for not being a true wife, but a concubine; which, notwithstanding, he did not do. It is, likewise, recorded, that Leo V. when he understood, that a certain bishop, in Africa, had two wives, he only decreed, that, by reason of the words of Paul, *he should be degraded and deprived of his office*? but *not* that *he should be obliged to divorce his second wife, or be in any other way punished on account of his bigamy.* Gregorius, also Bishop of Rome, writing to Bonifacius, who was sent into Germany to teach Christianity, not more than one hundred and twenty one years after Christ's birth, beseeches him, to *take care, that such as had espoused a plurality of women, and had buried all except one, might content themselves with that one, and not take any other.* So that he only *exhorts* men to abstain from polygamy, just as he might *exhort* them to celibacy; which cannot be accepted by any but such as, by the ALMIGHTY, are called to that state of life. The true Ecclesiastical Canons, which oblige us to their observance, are such as are grounded on the Divine Word. But, to convince you, read the Epistle written by Gregorius III, Bishop of Rome, to the above cited Bonifacius, where you shall find him saying to this purpose, *viz.*

If any man has a wife, who, by reason of some bodily infirmity, cannot afford to her husband due benevolence, he shall do well to abstain from her: But if he cannot contain (for that is the Gift of GOD, not given to all) it is better he should marry another wife, than burn; provided he allows his former wife all necessary maintenance. Than this, what can be more clearly expressed?

Ochy. All you can utter, should you plead till doomsday, will never convince me, that it is either decent, reasonable, or lawful for a man to have more than a single wife.

Tely. Set the case, that the number of women does everywhere exceed that of men, what must become of the poor unmated women?

Ochy. They must take the same course as the men should do, if the number of men exceeded: That is: Pray to GOD to bestow on them the Gift of Continence.

Tely. In case GOD calls, to a married state, a man who has not the least portion of that Gift of Continence, so requisite to a single life, it would be but in vain for him to pray for the Gift of being rendered able to live without a wife; for I am of the opinion, he would not obtain his request, since GOD calls him to marry.

Ochy. The whole Christian World has believed polygamy to be unlawful; nor can any man have more than one wife, without giving all imaginable offence, which by all ought carefully to be avoided. Besides, GOD wills us, to be obedient to our magistrates: And they are so far from allowing polygamy, that they will put to death the man who is proved to have two wives.

Tely. But not, if he keeps about him a whole troop of whores! If any man, being, by instinct Divine, moved to marry diverse women, and his so doing should be no sin, if he married them, it were, as the saying goes, a *scandal taken,* and not *given.* Also, to avoid scandal, he might marry his second wife privately.

Ochy. Such matters are, however, scarcely practicable: And if he should be seen frequently in his second wife's company, the world would take offence, as judging her to be his concubine. I shall therefore, continually persevere in exhorting men to shun polygamy; and I heartily dehort you from thinking on it. Even the Romish clergy make vows of perpetual celibacy: And shall we, who are men Regenerate, Spiritual and Evangelical, think of entertaining a diversity of wives!

Tely. Right! And how chastely those single livers pass their vowed celibacy, all the world knows, and observes. The Law itself condemns unfruitful matrimony; so far is it from not condemning spontaneous unfruitful celibacy. Now, I speak expressly of such as are not called to a single life. The ancient Romans used to punish those who lived unmarried, and rewarded such as augmented the commonwealth by a numerous progeny. The like was also decreed by Lycurgus and Ulpianus. Now, what can merit a greater benediction than the preservation of mankind, which, were it not for matrimony, would be utterly annihilate? A man cannot transmit to posterity a more honorable memorial of his name, than by leaving behind him children virtuously educated. And what greater folly can be imagined, than, under a show of holiness, to shun holy matrimony, as a thing profane, which, nevertheless, has been ordained by GOD; is dictated by nature; is persuaded by reason; was confirmed by Christ; has been, and is, praised by writers, sacred and profane; authorized by all laws; unanimously approved by all nations! and whereunto we are invited by the example of the best men? On the other hand; What more inhumanly barbarous, than to hate matrimony, the desire whereof we have in us implanted by nature? What more ungratefully unthankful to nature, the world, and our own species, than not to beget children, as our ancestors and parents have begot us? For my part, I make account, that such men are murderers of as many as they might have begotten had they embraced matrimony; except, peradventure, they are carried by a Divine impulse to lead a single life. Without question, it is a sort of manslaughter, not only to cause abortion or sterility by drugs, or the like, but also to shun matrimony, without a very just cause.

Ochy. I am not condemning matrimony, namely, the having one wife; but the having two, or more.

Tely. But what is it you will advise me to do?

Ochy. To think no more of marrying any more wives, but to pray to GOD for the Gift of Continence.

Tely. What, if He will not give it me;

Ochy. He will, if you pray in faith.

Tely. What, if He neither gives me the Gift, nor the faith to ask it?

Ochy. If you then do that to which GOD shall incline you, so that you are sure that you are led by Divine instigation, you shall not err. For it can be no error to obey GOD. Other advice I cannot give you. Therefore, I bid you farewell; and promise you, that I will seek the LORD in your behalf.

Tely. And that is what I beseech you to do, that I may not offend GOD; but that I may give Him all honor and glory, through CHRIST our LORD, *Amen.*

FINIS

ON
POLYGAMY.
A
DIALOGUE.

By BARN. OCHINO.

T. I Am come to requeſt a little of your Advice; as conceiving you want neither Will nor Ability to afford it me: Wherefore to you it is that I chuſe to addreſs myſelf.

O. Willing I moſt certainly am to give it you; and alſo ready; provided it be nothing beyond the Reach of my Capacity.

T. What I intreat you, in the firſt Place, is, that you faithfully-promiſe to keep my Council.

B. That

T. Telypolygamus   *O. Ochinus*

O. That you may depend on, if you advance not any thing tending to God's Dishonour.

T. I have a Wife, who so little suits with my Fancy, that I cannot by any Means relish her; and, so far as I can hitherto perceive, she is not only barren, but unhealthy. Now, such is my Disposition, that I cannot be without a Woman's Company; and am also desirous of having Children, as well for Posterity-Sake, as for the Pleasure I should take in educating my Off-spring in the Fear of God. I might, indeed, keep a Concubine, or two: But that my Conscience will not suffer me to do. Nay, I might wrongfully charge my Wife with Adultery; and so get rid of her: But, in doing that, I should not only grievously offend the Almighty, but blemish my own and the poor Woman's Reputation, neither of which can I prevail with myself to offer at. One might likewise make her away by some Dose: But of that I abhor even the very Mention. Yet a Thought is come into my Head, which may make me easy; and that is, in plain Terms, to marry another Wife, without parting from her I have already: And this, according to my Conception, God himself has put into my Mind, and that, by Him, I am thereunto called. My Desire, therefore, is,

T. Telypolygamus   *O. Ochinus*

On POLYGAMY.

is, that you will resolve me, whether according to his Word, I may not lawfully do it?

O. In Cases dubious, my Friend, Advice is very requisite. But, certainly, no Case can be more evident, than that a Man ought not to have more Wives than one at once; the very Condition of Marriage being such, that it cannot be between more than two.

T. How is it you make that appear?

O. At the Beginning our Creator made, out of *Adam*, one Woman only, and gave her to him; signifying thereby, *that he ought to have but one, and that Matrimony ought to be but of two Persons only.* Had it been his Divine Pleasure, that a Man should have had a Plurality of Women, doubtless he would have created more than one, especially in the World's Infancy, when Propagation was so much more necessary than for ever after.

T. This Argument, I conceive to be but of slender Validity. GOD, you say, gave to our Grandsire *Adam* one Wife; and therefore it is not lawful for any of his Male Posterity to have more.

O. Had it been, I say again, his Creator's Will, that he should have had more, he would have given him more, especially at that Time of Perfection in which he had vouchsafed to state him.

T.

T. Telypolygamus   *O. Ochinus*

T. A mere Act of God, without any Precept thereunto annexed, does not absolutely injoin us to a strict Imitation of the same: Since, if so, we should be obliged to wear no other Garments but Skins, because God so cloathed our primitive Parents, and consequently our dressing ourselves in Cloth, Silk, &c. is unlawful. At that Rate your Argument would always be of Force: God cloathed them with Skins, and could have cloathed them with Cloth, or Silk, had it been his Pleasure that Mankind should have been so cloathed. If an Act of God does as much bind us as a Precept, so that God's giving to *Adam* one Wife only was, in Effect, as much as if he had said; *I will and command, that each Man shall have only one Wife*, it must follow, that not only it would be illegal for a Man to have more Wives than one, but likewise, that every Man who does not take to him a Wife (having it in his Power so to do) is guilty of the Sin of Disobedience; which is repugnant to St. *Paul's* Doctrine.

O. You are to take Notice, that the Apostle does not, in any Respect, go contrary to God's Proceeding. God gave only one Wife to *Adam*: And that was the same as if he had expresly said; *I will, that a Man have not more Wives than one: And it is my Pleasure he shall have one, except I call him to a Single*

T. Telypolygamus *O. Ochinus*

On POLYGAMY.

Single Life, by bestowing on him the Gift of Chastity. And this is St. *Paul's* Intent and Meaning. 1 *Cor.* 7.

T. And I, for my Part, must say, that when GOD gave to *Adam* one Wife, it was as if he had said; *It is my Pleasure, that a Man shall have one Wife, if either he wants the Gift of Continence, or I shall call him to a Married Condition. It is also my Pleasure, that he shall have no more, except he stands in need of more, or I shall call him to more.* Which is, at this present, my very Condition, who stand in *need of*, and am *called* to marry another.

O. That a Single Life is pleasing to GOD, the Word of GOD evidences: But we are not thereby taught, that He is pleased Men should have more than one Wife.

T. Nay, verily, both the Word of GOD, and the Example of Saints, teach the same, as shall presently be demonstrated. Mean while, let us, pre-suppose, that it had been the ALMIGHTY's Will that every Man should have as many Wives as he could possibly manage and govern, together with their Children; how many Wives must *Adam* have had given him, whereby to signify the Donor's Pleasure, in this Point?

O. You are supposing what cannot be Since the having more Wives than one is utterly repugnant to the very Essence of real Matrimony. *T.*

T. Telypolygamus   *O. Ochinus*

T. Hitherto, you have not cleared it up to me, that the having more than one Wife is repugnant to Marriage, otherwise than by saying, *that* God *gave to* Adam *one, and no more.* Let us now suppose he had given him more than one. Assuredly, from that original Instance you could not make good, that a Man ought not to have any more than *Adam* had. I say, therefore, in such a Case; how many Wives must God, of Necessity, have given to *Adam*, in order to signify the Divine Pleasure, in this Point?

O. Two would have been very sufficient.

T. Now, if that Act of God's had been a Precept, as you would urge, it would then have been unlawful for Men to have had either more or less than two Wives; which, nevertheless, would not have been conformable to his Will, seeing his Intent was, that they should have as many as they were capable of managing: Otherwise it would be sinful in a Minister to celebrate the Lord's Supper, except the Communicants were exactly in Number so many, and no more, as were *Christ*'s Apostles, when the same was first instituted.

O. Notwithstanding, it does not necessarily follow, that, because God gave to *Adam* one Wife, it is therefore unlawful for a Man to have more; yet it, doubtless, is a very specious Argument to persuade, nay, urges
strongly,

T. Telypolygamus *O. Ochinus*

strongly, though it be not wholly compulsive.

T. Nay, nay; it urges not at all: Since it may be alledged, that God gave to *Adam* one Wife, not to signify it to be his Will, that each Man should have one only Wife, but rather, that all Mankind in general, having proceeded as well from one Mother as one Father, should so much the more love and effect each other: Also that *Eve*, being formed of *Adam*'s Rib, might be a Type of the Holy *Mother* Church, the only *Spouse* of *Christ*.

O. Well, but let us now draw nearer to the Words of the Text. Think you not, that *Adam* was moved by an Instinct Divine, when he said; *For this Cause shall a Man* leave *his* Father *and* Mother, *and* cleave *unto his* Wife?

T. Doubtless he was.

O. And do you not observe, that in saying, *a Man shall* cleave *to his Wife*, not *Wives*, he instructs us, that a Man is to have but *One?*

T. Mighty well: And, pray, when God commands a Man to *love* his *Neighbour*, does he oblige him to *love* but *one*, or *more?*

O. All his Neighbours in general.

T. That is not so: For he expresly says, *Love* thy *Neighbour*, not thy *Neighbours*; therefore

T. Telypolygamus   *O. Ochinus*

therefore, whoever loves *one* of his *Neighbours*, does fulfil that Injunction.

O. Chrift, when he said; *Love thy Neighbour*, spake it in this Sense, as if he should have said; *Thou shalt* love every one *of thy* Neighbours.

T. So likewise *Adam* when he said; *He shall* cleave *unto his* Wife, intimated, that he should *cleave* unto *every Woman* who was his *Wife:* And therefore, from those Words, it cannot be made out, That it is unlawful for a Man to have more than one Wife.

O. But what can you have to say to those Words of his which follow; *And of them* twain *shall be made one Flesh?* For he says, not of *three* or *four*. From these Words it is undoubtedly manifest, that he designed not that Marriage should be made between more than two Persons.

T. Adam says not, *Of* them twain *shall be made* one *Flesh*; but, *They shall be made one Flesh.*

O. But that certainly was his Meaning, as plainly appears from the Words of *Chrift*; who, quoting the said Speech, says; *That* GOD, *by* Adam, *declared, that they* two *shall be one Flesh*; adding this Clause; *They are no longer* two, *but* one *Flesh.*

T. That is, as if he had said; *The Husband shall love every one as his Wives as if she were the same Flesh, and the same Body*
with

T. Telypolygamus   *O. Ochinus*

with him; and so, in like manner, shall every Wife love her Husband.

O. But GOD said, *They two shall be* one; therefore they cannot be *three* or *four*.

T. Your Argument would hold Water, had he said, *They two* only *shall be one.* And so, as all this is of no Force, *Christ* says, *Mat.* xviii. *If two of you, on Earth, shall agree about a Thing, they shall obtain what they ask.* Therefore, if three or four shall agree, they shall not obtain what they ask. So is this no sound Inference. GOD said; *They* two *shall be* one *Flesh:* Wherefore, if the Parties be three, it is not true Marriage.

O. It is humanly impossible for more than *two* to become *one* Flesh.

T. In the Primitive Church, there were not only two Believers, but they were in very great Numbers, having, nevertheless, but one Heart, one Mind: Yet you believe, that, if a Man has diverse Wives, he cannot become one Flesh with them. *If a Man, while he cleaves to a Harlot, becomes,* as St. *Paul* says, *one Body with her, notwithstanding he has a Wife, should he not much more become one Flesh with her, if he makes her his Wife?*

O. Say what you will; to have more than one Wife is a Thing filthy, dishonest and quite contrary, nay destructive to the holy State of Matrimony.

B 5 *T.*

T. Telypolygamus   *O. Ochinus*

T. And yet *Abraham*, you know, had more Wives than one; as likewise *David*, and abundance of others, under the *Old Law*. And had it been unlawful for them to have taken to them more than one Wife, they would have been Sinners in marrying several Women; and what Children they had by all their Wives, except the first, would have been Bastards, because not begot in lawful Matrimony.

O. Much sooner will I grant all this, than I will allow, or grant it to be a legal Thing, for a Man to entertain more than one Wife. Those Ancients were pious, good Men, yet were they sometimes guilty of Sins. They were frail Sinners, as being born of *Adam*, as appears in the Example of *David*: And it would have been deceiving themselves, to have denied their being Sinners.

T. That they sometimes sinned, I shall easily grant. But I will never yield, that they continued in their Sins till their Death; which yet they certainly did, in case it was unlawful for them to have several Wives: Whence it would follow, that they were all Damned, as are those who die while they persevere in entertaining Concubines. As for us, we cannot hold them for Saints, since we know not, for certain, that they ever repented. *David* having perpetrated those Sins

---

T. Telypolygamus   *O. Ochinus*

On POLYGAMY.

Sins of Adultery and Murder, the LORD, becaufe he was one of his Elect, fent to him his Prophet, to reprove him; as, likewife, when he numbered the People, contrary to GOD's Command. It is, therefore, very credible, that, had the having diverfe Wives been a Breach of Divine Law, GOD would have ufed the like Proceedings towards him, that he might have avoided Eternal Perdition. But perufe the Scripture throughout, yet you will not find one Syllable of GOD's having prohibited a Plurality of Wives: Nor is it probable that, had it been contrary to the Law of GOD, *Mofes* would ever have diffembled the Matter. Nay, and the Scripture informs us, *that David was a Man after* GOD's *own Heart*; and that, *fo long as he lived, he was obedient to all the* LORD's *Commandments*; excepting only in *Uriah*'s Affair. So that, had it been a Sin to have diverfe Wives, and feeing, alfo, that it was a Matter fufficiently known, and far from being a private Practife, the Writer would have excepted againft it, or he muft make himfelf a Lyar, by faying, *That* David *committed only that Sin of* Homicide, *under which his* Adultery *is comprehended*. Then again, how could that be true, which GOD faid to *David*, when, blaming him for his Unthankfulnefs, He told him; *That He had*

had given *him* many Wives; who, doubtless, must have been all *Whores*, except the first; and so it must not have been GOD, but the *Devil,* who gave them to him. Moreover, you will there find GOD to have made a Law; *That if any Man had two Wives, the one beloved, the other hated, and by them had diverse Children, and of whom the eldest Male was born of the hated Woman, the Father should not be allowed to make the Son of his beloved Wife his Heir.* Now it might happen, that the beloved Woman was the first Wife, and so it might come to pass, that, tho' the Husband had Children by the latter sooner than by the former, yet, were your Assertions just, they would be Bastards, as being born of a Whore, and consequently incapable of being Heirs. By the Word of GOD it is, therefore, true, that all the Children are alike legitimate, tho' sprung from diverse Wives, by one and the same Husband; and that, therefore, not only the first, but all the succeeding Marriages are lawful, seeing GOD himself did approve and bless them, in those holy Men the Patriarchs, or primitive Fathers of the World.

O. The first Consequence of my Opinion is, you say, *That all who died actually possessed of a Plurality of Wives, must needs be Damned.* To this I answer, *That,*
in

in case they died, not having put away all but the first Wife, without repenting of that their Sin, in particular, they absolutely are Damned: But such of them as are Saved, did repent of the Sin, and divorce all, except the first, and only lawful Wife.

T. But is it not apparent, that ever any did so; and yet, if your Opinion were true, Mention ought to be made thereof in Sacred Writ, whereby we might be given to understand, that to have a Plurality of Wives is a detestable Abomination.

O. It already was sufficiently known, that Men ought not to have any more than only one Wife, by reason that God had ordained, that the Husband and Wife should, of two, become one Flesh.

T. Far is it from being likely, that it was not lawful to have several Wives, and that the Unlawfulness thereof was known, yet that *Abraham, Jacob, David,* with other worthy Persons like them, should nevertheless openly marry more Wives than one.

O. That is really very good! As if many good, pious People, in ancient Times, did not sin, tho' they knew what they were doing to be unlawful.

T. But they did not persevere in those Sins to their Lives End, as did those who entertained a Plurality of Wives.

O. I

T. Telypolygamus   *O. Ochinus*

O. I told you before, that, *if they were of* God's *Elect, they did at last repent.*

T. But then, we ought not any longer to account those Patriarchs for Saints, and quote them for Patterns of Goodness and Piety, seeing we are assured of their having sinned, as you urge, by having a Diversity of Wives, but we have not any Assurance at all of their having repented.

O. True; unless the Word of God assures us that they were Saints: As for Example, we know *Abraham, Isaac* and *Jacob* to be Saints, because *Christ* says, that *many should come from the* East, *and from the* West, *and sit down, with* Abraham, Isaac *and* Jacob, *in the Kingdom of Heaven.* Now, I conclude, that *Moses* permitted the *Jews*, because of the Hardness of their Hearts, to put away their Wives without just Cause; so likewise, for the same Reason, he suffered them to have several Wives; that is to say, *he did not hinder, nor forbid it, nor punish the same, by any Law enact in his Commonwealth.* But it does not, therefore, follow, that they did not sin in the Sight of God; nor that they deserved not Punishment, unless they repented.

T. Those Things are all permitted, which are neither hindered, forbid, nor punished. Truly, I will not say *Moses* sinned, if, to avoid a greater Evil, and to com-

comport with the *Jews* Hardness of Heart, he permitted them to have sundry Wives; that is to say, *he neither hindered, nor punished them:* But, if he permitted them so as not even to forbid it them, I cannot say but that he did sin. For, *Moses* ought expresly to have forbidden, that any Man should have more than one Wife; which because he has not any where done, we must needs conclude, that it is not a Thing unlawful.

O. Plurality of Wives was then, as it is now, so apparently vicious, filthy, and indecent, that it was needless for *Moses* to forbid it.

T. And was it not as apparent, that Adultery was a Thing vicious, filthy, and indecent? Yea, incomparably more so than Diversity of Wives: Yet he very expresly forbad Adultery. But, in case it had been unlawful to have sundry Wives, he ought to have inhibited *that* so much the more expresly, by how much the Unlawfulness thereof was less manifest than was the Unlawfulness of Adultery. Is it not a clear Case, that Murder is unlawful? Yet he forbids that. In short; what are the Ten Commandments, but an express Epitome of the Laws of Nature?

O. It might be said, that GOD *might remit the Transgressions against the Second* Table,

T. Telypolygamus   *O. Ochinus*

ble, *because He is not only above all Creatures, but above his own Law:* And, perhaps, He might remit the same to all Mankind, born before the Death of *Christ*, and, consequently, be willing they should have a Diversity of Wives, without Sin: And so it comes to pass, that they, under the *Old Law*, who had more Wives than one, did not sin; and, under that Consideration, God might give many Wives to *David*. Tho' it may, likewise, be said, that He gave them to him only thus; He permitted him to have them, inasmuch as He neither hindered, nor punished him.

T. If your Assertion be just, that the Unlawfulness of entertaining more than one Wife is clear from the Word of God, who said, *that* two *should be made* one *Flesh*; yet that God did so far remit of his Laws, that Men should not sin in having more, does not appear in God's Word: That Opinion of yours, therefore, has not any good Foundation.

O. If you will but recollect well, you will find, that *Lamech*, a very wicked Man, was the first who had two Wives. Other pious Men, who preceded him, knowing the Will of God, had only each of them one Wife.

T. As if *Abraham*, *Isaac* and *Jacob*, were not holier Men than any of those you hint

---

T. Telypolygamus   *O. Ochinus*

On POLYGAMY.

hint at! But, in the firſt Place, I am at a Loſs to divine, how you came to be ſo poſitive that *Lamech* was the firſt Man who had two Wives; he is, indeed, the firſt mentioned in Scripture to have had two. But as this is a vain Argument; ſo, ſince the Scripture does not any where mention *Cain*'s having more than one Son, muſt it therefore be an undiſputable Conſequence, that he had no more? Nor is the following leſs vain. It is not any where in Scripture recorded, that thoſe Men who lived before *Lamech* had more Wives than one: *Ergo*, none of them had more than one Wife. Moreover, where it is ſaid, that *Lamech* had two Wives, it is not charged on him as a Sin, or Crime, but ſeems rather to be intimated as a Thing pleaſing in GOD's Eye, that a Man ſhould have more Wives than one; ſeeing, by them, He gave to *Lamech* ſuch ingenious Sons, who became the Inventors of Arts and Sciences, not only delightful but profitable. Neither can I perceive, how you came to be informed, that *Lamech* was ſo very wicked a Man as you would inſinuate.

O. GOD plagued him, by ſuffering him to fall into the Sins of Murder and Deſpair, merely on Account of his having married two Wives.

T. For

T. For my Part, I cannot conceive him to have been either a Murderer, or that he fell into Despair, nor are we taught any thing like all that by the Scriptures, if they are rightly interpreted; or even had the Scripture intimated any such Matter, which I do not grant, yet can it not from thence appear, that God suffered him so to go astray, purely for having married two Wives.

O. But, we may reasonably conjecture, that his having two Wives was displeasing to God; since the said Murder is mentioned presently after.

T. First, I have told you already, that, by the Words of that Text, if they be understood rightly, there is not any sound Implication either of his Homicide, or Despair: And even if such were ever so plainly demonstrated, I say, it does not therefore follow, that his Diversity of Wives was the Occasion, or that God was offended with him on that Account; inasmuch as, immediately on the Mention of his two Wives, the Lord commends their Sons; as if He would have us to understand, that He approves of such Plurality of Wives. Add to this, that nothing ought to be affirmed, or asserted, in God's Church, as necessary to Salvation, if it be

not

T. Telypolygamus   *O. Ochinus*

not otherwife to be known than barely by Conjecture.

O. Seeing I am not like to convince you from the *Old Teftament*, I will try what is to be done with you from the *New Law*.

T. You err, if you judge the *Old Law* not to be fufficient to teach every Article of what is neceffary to Salvation. If therefore that be your Reafon for having Recourfe to the *New Teftament*, you are deceived: Seeing, as St. *Paul* writes; *All Scripture, of Divine Infpiration, is profitable for Reprehenfion, Correction and Inftruction in Righteoufnefs, that the* Man of God *may be made perfect, furnifhed for every good Work.* Now, it is clear, that *Paul*, in that Place, fpeaks of thofe Scriptures wherein *Timothy* had been exercifed from his Infancy: And, becaufe the *New Law* was then written, you muft be forced to acknowledge, that *Paul*, there, fpeaks of the *Old Teftament.* The *Old Law*, therefore, is profitable, not only to affert the Truth of fuch Things as are neceffary to Salvation, but likewife to confute Falfities; and, confequently to render a Man perfect: For which Caufe, *Chrift*, fpeaking thereof, fays; *Search the Scriptures, for in them is found Eternal Life.*

O. Per-

T. Telypolygamus   *O. Ochinus*

O. Perhaps, some certain Things are prohibited to us, in the *New Testament*, which were not forbidden in the *Old*.

T. In Matters of Morality, whatever is unlawful, and to us prohibited, was in like Manner evermore forbidden to them; and also, whatever was allowed and commanded to them, the same is likewise allowed and commanded to us. GOD was equally Author of the *Old Testament* and of the *New*; nor was He ever contrary, or unlike to Himself.

O. We may say, *That some Things were allowed to those under the* Old *Law, because of their Imperfection, which are not allowed to us, in whom Carnalities should be abundantly more curbed and mortified.*

T. You take for granted what you have not proved; *viz.* That it is unlawful to have more than one Wife. Nay again, you are in the Wrong, if you hold it to be bad to have one Wife, but worse to have two: For as the Matrimonial Act, in him who has one Wife, is a Thing not in itself evil, nor repugnant to those Actions which are necessary to Salvation, no more is it evil to have two, or more Wives, provided a Man has a *Call* from *Above* to marry them, and is moved, not merely by the Impulse of the *Flesh*, but of the *Spirit*, that he may have Children, and bring them

them up in the Fear of GOD; his Wives also doing the fame. Whence it follows, that he who has two, or more Wives, may be as perfect as he who has but one, or none. Nor had *Abraham*, becaufe he had fundry Wives, a fcantier Portion of Faith, Hope, or Charity than Priefts, Monks, or Friers, who marry not at all. Conjugal Chaftity is as well the Gift of GOD as is that of Celibacy. For this Caufe, St. *Paul* faid; *Every one is endowed with his Gift from* GOD, *fome one Way, fome another*. 2 Cor. 7.

O. In that Place, the Apoftle exhorted the *Corinthians* to a Single Life; and that for no other Reafon, than becaufe a Married State has many Incumberances attending it: Inafmuch as Married People, being intangled with Worldly Affairs, are not fo free to pray and preach up and down, and do good to others, as are thofe who are Single. Now, if the having one Wife brings along with it fo many Impediments, one may readily conjecture, what a Plurality of Wives will do. *Ergo*, to have more than one, is abfolutely unlawful.

T. You are in an Error, if you imagine, that St. *Paul*'s Meaning, in thofe Words, was, that Marriage impeded Men in their Journey Heavenwards, fo that Married People could not be Saved: For then what

T. Telypolygamus   *O. Ochinus*

what God said would not be true; *viz.* That *it was not good for a Man to be alone*. But it would rather be most meritoriously excellent to be alone, and to marry at all, would be the vilest Deed one could do, as being a Mortal Sin. So far from that, I cannot but hold, that a Married Man may not only be Saved as well as a Single One, but also be as compleatly perfect as he; inasmuch as he may attain to as great Perfection, in Faith, Hope, and Charity, as the other: And if he cannot personally perform some external Works, which the Batchelor can, as impeded by his Matrimonial Incumberances, yet he may perform the same in Heart and Mind; which is what God most regards.

O. Tho' Matrimony itself does not deprive a Man of a future Felicity, yet his having more Wives than one, does.

T. How prove you that?

O. From *Paul*; who, speaking of Bishops, says; *He would have them be the Husbands of one Wife*: Meaning, that they should not have more. It is therefore unlawful to have more Wives than one.

T. Nay; rather when he tells them, expresly by Name, that *one Wife they should have, lest, having more, they should be too much incumbered with Mundane Affairs*, it is easy to comprehend, that he allowed other Men to have more. *O.* St.

T. Telypolygamus   *O. Ochinus*

On POLYGAMY.

O. St. *Paul*'s Mind is, by some, interpreted, *A Bishop is to have but one Wife*; *that is,* say they, *the Church* for his *Spiritual Spouse.*

T. Many Reasons demonstrate this to be a very false Opinion. First; because *Christ* is only the Spouse of Souls, and Bridegroom of his Church: And if we, who are Ministers, be his Friends, we ought, with *John* the *Baptist*, as the Friends of *Christ*, the only true Spouse of Souls, to send them to him, their Bridegroom; and not to draw them to ourselves. *Christ*'s Churches, therefore, are not the Bishops Spouses: And if they were, as a Husband is his Wife's Superior, so should they be to their respective Churches; against which writes *Paul* to the *Corinthians*, where his Words are; *We are not Lords over your Faith, or over you by reason of your Faith.* The Church, therefore, is not *Paul*'s Wife. I confess, indeed, that one Church is sufficient for one Pastor; and he merits no small Praise, if he can govern that as it ought to be governed. In the ancient Times of *Christianity*, one Church had sometimes diverse Pastors, as appears from the *Epistle* to the *Philippians*, in which *Paul* salutes the Bishops who were at *Philippi*: Whereas now-a-Days, one Bishop has many Churches. Also, when *Paul*

T. Telypolygamus   *O. Ochinus*

Paul says; *A Bishop ought to have one Wife:* he speaks of the Manners of him who was fit to be a Bishop: But in case he be yet to be chosen, he is no Bishop; and therefore, as yet, has no Church which may be called his Wife. From hence, likewise, it is manifest, that, by Wife, he did not mean Church; because, almost presently after those Words, he makes Mention of his Children, ordaining, that *he govern well his Family, and keep his Children in Subjection to him, with all due Reverence.* For if a Man cannot govern his own Family, how can he preside over GOD's Church? Wherefore, in that Place, he assuredly speaks of a Wife, and not of a Church.

O. Some affirm, that *Paul,* there, forbids such Men to be chosen Bishops as have had more than one Wife, tho' not at one Time.

T. Yet I cannot conceive, that *Paul* deemed it a Sin for a Man, after the Decease of his First Wife, to take to him a Second; forasmuch as he himself says; *That after the Husband's Death, the Wife is free, and may, without Blame, marry another.* So far is it from being unlawful for a Man, after the Death of one Wife, to espouse another.

O. I

T. Telypolygamus   *O. Ochinus*

On POLYGAMY.

O. It is held to be a very enormous Shame, for a Man to marry again when his firſt Wife is dead.

T. If you rightly weigh the Matter, and follow not the Opinions of the blind, ſenſeleſs Vulgar, you will find the Matrimonial Act to be as free from any Turpitude, as the Acts of Eating and Drinking: Nor would GOD have injoined Matrimony, had it been evil; which, nevertheleſs, he expreſly did, when he ſaid, *Increaſe and Multiply.*

O. I condemn not Matrimony; but the Iteration, or Repetition thereof.

T. The ſecond Nuptials are as true and valid as the firſt: And therefore you cannot condemn the Iteration of Matrimony, without condemning alſo Matrimony itſelf. Take one Inſtance. A young Man marries a Wife; ſhe dies a few Days after; he is naturally incontinent, or has a ſecond Call to the Matrimonial State: In this Caſe, who is ignorant, that, anſwerably to the very Precept of *Paul*, ſince he cannot contain, he may and ought to take another Wife?

O. Were not ſecond Marriages filthy and unlawful, *Paul* would not, ſpeaking afterwards of Widows, have commanded ſuch to be choſen as had not had more than one Huſband.

T. Con-

T. Telypolygamus   *O. Ochinus*

T. Conceive you *Paul* to have been a Perſon inclined to Superſtition?

O. I do not conceive him to have been ſuch.

T. Had a ſprightly young Widow, ſomewhat incontinent, applied herſelf to *Paul*, for his Advice; what think you his Anſwer would have been?

O. That ſhe ſhould re-marry; according to his Doctrine and Precept.

T. Repeated Marriages are not, therefore, unlawful. Why, then, ſhould *Paul* reject ſuch Widows as had been married oftener than once? For it was very poſſible, that ſome Widows, having had diverſe Huſbands, might be infinitely chaſter, and more pious than thoſe who had wedded only one. It might alſo happen, that ſhe who had ſeveral Huſbands, might have lived with them only one Year; whereas ſhe who had one only Huſband, might have co-habited with him thirty or forty Years: And in ſuch Caſe, I cannot really ſee, why *this* ſhould be worthier to be choſen, than *that*. My Belief, therefore, is, that *Paul*'s Mind, in that Place, was this; *That ſuch Widows were not to be choſen as had been divorced from ſeveral Huſbands, and had married in the Life-times of thoſe Huſbands from whom they were divorced:* For they were either divorced on juſt Grounds, and

and it was not fit they should be chosen, or on unjust Grounds, and so the Marriage remained good, having never been violated, and the divorced Woman had committed a Sin if she married another: Hence it was, that all divorced Women were counted infamous, not only such as married again to others, but, likewise, such as abstained from Wedlock, especially among the *Gentiles*, who used not to divorce their Wives, except for some Fault, or vicious Quality. *Paul*, therefore, did not ever condemn those Women who re-married after the Decease of a former Husband; neither did he prohibit those Men to be Bishops, who married another Woman when their former Wife was dead; which, nevertheless, the superstitious *Papists* observe, because they understand not *Paul*'s Meaning. Among them, tho' a Man has entertained ever so many Strumpets, they make him a Bishop; but, his First Wife being dead, if he marry another, they absolutely will not: Whence it comes to pass, that Matrimony with them, is of a worse Report, and far more scandalous, than either Fornication, Adultery, Incest, Sacrilege, Sodomy, or any other the most execrable Abominations one can imagine. *Paul*'s Mind (as has been observed concerning Widows, and this will make the third Opinion) is, *That he who has*

has had diverse Wives, by reason he divorced one, ought not to be made a Bishop: For if he divorced her unjustly, he ought not to be made a Bishop, in that Regard; if justly, yet his Wife's Infamy, redounding on himself, does that Way incapacitate him; And on this Account it was, that *Paul* would not agree he should be a Bishop. Nevertheless, I cannot favour these Sentiments: For, he says not; he must *have been*; but says; he must *be* the Husband of one Wife; for he says; he must be blameless, *viz.* as the Husband of one Wife; as he expresses it, a little after, with Relation to Deacons, and writing to *Titus* concerning Bishops.

O. By Reason that Bishops, in Regard of the Public Office they bear, as also Deacons, have Dealings with all Sorts of Persons, not only Men but Women, *Paul*, to avoid Suspicion, would have them to be married: And this, perhaps, might be the Meaning of those Words. It may, likewise, possibly be that the Apostle, foreseeing the future *Papistical* Superstition, prohibiting the Marriage of Bishops, *&c.* that they might be without Excuse, said; *They ought to be blameless, and to have a Wife:* But, indeed, he did not expresly say, *they are to have one only, and no more.* Or he shews, that a Bishop should have a Wife, that is, he

should

T. Telypolygamus *O. Ochinus*

should be satisfied with her, and not to have any Kind of unclean Dealings with other Women: All which is no other than injoining him to be chaste and honest.

T. *Paul*'s Mind here is, certainly, neither more nor less than thus : *That it is lawful for the Generality of* Christians *to have a Plurality of Wives* ; *but for each Bishop to have no more than one:* Not that it was sinful for them to have more ; but because the Duty of Bishops being to labour for the Salvation of others, he was apprehensive left a Multiplicity of Wives might be a Remora, or Obstacle to the due Performance of their Function. On this Account, he would not admit their having more than one ; nor is it, therefore, unlawful for other Men to have more: Nay, while he forbids Bishops and Deacons, by Name, to have a Plurality of Wives, he tacitly allows it to others. Nor is it at all likely, that *Paul* would have prohibited Bishops having more than one Wife, had it not been then usual for them to have more. It was, therefore, in the *New Testament* forbidden to Bishops to have a Plurality of Wives, as, in the *Old Testament*, it was forbidden to Kings *(Deut.* 17.) not because it was in itself unlawful, but left Kings, whose Office was of the greatest Consequence, being distracted by their Wives,

T. Telypolygamus   *O. Ochinus*

Wives should become corrupt; as it happened to *Soloman*: For if *Adam*, when he had but one, was, notwithstanding, perverted by her, it is easy to conjecture what might happen to Kings, if they had many. Nevertheless, I cannot but believe, that as, in the same Place, he forbad Kings to have many Horses, meaning, a too enormous Multitude of them; lest in them, rather than in GOD, they should put their Trust: For otherwise, the having many Horses was not disallowed. Even so, they were not forbid to have many Wives; since *David*, a most Holy Man, even one after GOD's own Heart, had several; but that they should not entertain any immoderate Multitude of Wives, more particularly of such as were professed *Heathens*, worshipping False Deities. But to return more closely to our Point: It is not credible, that *Paul* was apprehensive of *Timothy*'s electing for Bishops such as were unbaptized *Jews* or *Gentiles*: It is, therefore, plain, that, in *Christ*'s Church, among the Primitive *Christians*, there were Men who had more Wives than one; and because from among them a Bishop was to be chosen, he was against his making Choice of a Person who had a Plurality of Wives. But if to entertain more Wives than one had been, as you affirm it to be, repugnant to GOD's
LAW,

T. Telypolygamus   *O. Ochinus*

Law, and the firſt Wife only being rightful and legal, and the others all Harlots, it is not in the leaſt credible, that the *Chriſtian* Páſtors would have adminiſtered Baptiſm to any Man who had a Plurality of Wives, unleſs he put away all except his firſt: And had that been the Practiſe, it would have been very needleſs in *Paul* to ordain, that he who was to be choſen Biſhop ſhould be the Huſband of one only Wife; ſince the whole Community of *Chriſtians*, from among whom he was to be elected, had each of them no more than one. But what I much marvail at, is, that many, who not only firmly believe, but maintain in their Writings, *That it is utterly contrary to Law, both Moral and Natural to have more than one Wife*, do yet, in expounding *Paul*, affirm, *that, writing to* Timothy, *he cautions him not to chuſe for a Biſhop one who had a Plurality of Wives*; whence neceſſarily it follows, that, ſince Election was not to be made of any who was not within the Pale of *Chriſt*'s Church, the Church of *Chriſt* had within it ſuch as had more Wives than one, and conſequently did not think it unlawful to have more: Otherwiſe, had the *Chriſtians* counted it unlawful, as they did not baptize, or admit unto the Lord's Supper, any Man who entertained a Concubine, except he would for-

forsake her, so they would not have baptized, nor admitted to the Lord's Supper, nor even have suffered among them, such as had a Diversity of Wives, except they would divorce all but the first.

O. But what Reply can you make to *Paul*'s willing and commanding; *That every Man should have* his own Wife? For in saying, *his own Wife*, he certainly excludes *Wives*.

T. According to some, his Meaning is; *Let every Man have his own Wife:* That is, *his own*, not another Man's; and not, *one only*: As if a Father, pointing towards a Daughter of his, should say; *This is my own Daughter*; yet still not gainsaying, that he has other Daughters, which are also his *own*.

O. Paul does likewise, in the same Place, ordain; *That each Wife shall have her own* proper *Husband*; meaning such a Wife as is peculiar and proper to him alone, and not in common with other Wives: And hence it certainly follows, that as a Wife ought to be proper and peculiar to her Husband, and not to appertain to other Husbands, so the Husband ought to be appropriated to his first Wife, and not common to others, if you design (as you should do) so to expound *Paul*'s Text that he may not contradict himself.

T. Paul

T. Telypolygamus   *O. Ochinus*

On POLYGAMY.

T. *Paul* does not there difpute, a Man's having, or not having, a Plurality of Wives; but his Intent is to fhew, that thofe Men who have not the Gift of Continence, fhould take to them Wives; and that Women under the fame Circumftances fhould marry.

O. Can you, poffibly, not comprehend, that a Plurality of Wives is repugnant to the Matrimonial Contract, in which both Man and Woman reciprocally yield up to each other, during Life, the honeft Ufe of their refpective Bodies? On which Account, alfo, *Paul* fays; *That neither of them have Power over their own Bodies, but each over the other's refpectively*: And a Man having once granted the honeft Ufe of his Body to his Wife, he may not afterwards give the fame to any other, he having already given it up to the firft, who is become the rightful Owner thereof.

T. Yes, with the Confent of the firft he may; as did *Abraham*, when, by *Sa'rah*'s Permiffion, he went in unto *Hagar*; and confequently, with the Confent of his firft and fecond, a Man may marry a third; which is as right in other Men as in *Abraham*; efpecially where the Wives are given to underftand, that it is not finful for their Hufbands, with their Permiffion, to take to them other Wives.

T. Be-

T. Telypolygamus   *O. Ochinus*

O. Believe you, that *David*, when he espoused *Bathsheba*, had the Consent of his other Wives so to do, and that others who took to them a Diversity of Wives, did it with their former Wives Approbation?

T. Supposing they had it not; nevertheless their Marriages were as true and lawful as if otherwise: It being then a Matter universally known, and by Multitudes of Examples confirmed, that it was not any way unlawful for a Man to have several Wives: so that when, by Matrimony, a Man granted to his Wife the Use of his Body, he gave it not up to her so intirely as utterly to bereave himself of all Power to participate the same to other Wives; to all which the Wives, by the public Custom then in Force, were no Strangers, and tacitly acquiesced to it, since they knew their Husbands took them on those Conditions understood: Their Marriages, therefore, were lawful and valid.

O. No Man can marry a second Wife without wronging his first: Nor is it credible, that Wives did ever cordially consent to their Husbands doing them such manifest Injury as to marry others.

T. Possibly my Wife may prove barren; in which Case, it is absolutely her Duty to consent I take another; nay, of her own Accord, to advise me so to to do, as did *Sarah*: And should she disapprove thereof, she would therein do unjustly, and so her Husband may most legally espouse another Woman, in Spite of her unjust Opposition. Likewise, when a Wife is pregnant, and for some time after her Delivery, since she is then unfit for her Husband's Society, and also when she is distempered or aged, her Husband, without any Wrong done to her, may have Dealings with another Wife: Nay, though a Wife has no Ailing at all, and is apt for Procreation, yet ought she to be satisfied with having, at certain *meet* Times, the Enjoyment of her Husband's Society, and to leave him at free Liberty to distribute the rest of his Conversation, as he sees proper, among his other Wives.

O. May a Woman lawfully, think you, have a Plurality of Husbands?

T. Certainly, no.

O. Yet are there infirm Men, as well as there are ailing and distempered Women. Likewise can a Woman admit of Dealings with more Men, than a Man is able to have with Women: Wherefore it is seemingly more just, or at least less unjust, that a Woman should have a Plurality of Husbands, than that a Man should have several Wives.

T. Nay,

T. Telypolygamus *O. Ochinus*

T. Nay, nay; rather, seeing that Matrimony was ordained chiefly for Procreation-fake, and a Man having a Diverfity of Wives may, in a fhort Space of Time, have abundance more Children than can a Woman with diverfe Hufbands, it is undoubtedly more equitable for a Man to have many Wives, than for a Woman to have more than one Hufband. But the principal Reafons why Women ought not, by any Means, to be allowed a Diverfity of Hufbands, and yet Men may have diverfe Wives, are thefe: One, and the main Reafon of all, is that, by Women's having a Diverfity of Hufbands, the World would be nothing but Diforder, Diffention and Confufion; fince, as no Hufband could know, with any the leaft Certainty, the Off-fpring his Wife brings to be his own, he might always fufpect them to be another Man's, and of Confequence, would not take fuch Care of their Education and Welfare, as Hufbands now do, and with fome Reafon, as prefuming them to be his, though born of diverfe Wives; nay, very likely, being fo unaffured of their being his own Children, he would not appoint them to be his Heirs. Another Reafon why it is legal for Men to have feveral Wives, but not for Women to have a Diverfity of Hufbands, is this: A Hufband is his
Wife's

T. Telypolygamus   *O. Ochinus*

On POLYGAMY.

Wife's Head, and has over her Command and Authority, as being her Superior; for which Cause he may have many Wives, if he is in a Capacity of managing, instructing, and entertaining them as he ought: Nor is it any Way monstrous, but rather very comely, to have several Members to a Body, tho' but one Head; but a Body which has more than one Head, is a Monster: So for one Husband to have diverse Wives, is not at all monstrous; but for one Wife to have a Diversity of Husbands, is most monstrous. Wherefore, as there, unavoidably, would be Discord and Confusion for one Body to have more than one Head, and those Heads dissent in Opinion, as might well be; so would there be horrible Dissentions, Feuds and Inconveniences, if Wives had a Diversity of Husbands; since the Husbands might have contrary Minds, and lay on their Wives Injunctions quite different one from the other.

O. If we regard Discords and Inconveniencies, we shall find them sometimes to have been excessive, on account of a Man's having two Wives; as appears by the Stories of *Sarah* and *Hagar*, *Leah* and *Rachel*, *Hannah* and *Peninnah*, and several others, among whom reigned perpetual Dissentions: The which, possibly, the Almighty did

T. Telypolygamus   *O. Ochinus*

did permit, as a Token of his Difpleafure at Men's having a Plurality of Wives.

T. Though between the Firft-born and their Brethren, grievous Quarrels and Hatred have frequently arifen, as in *Cain* and *Abel,* in *Efau* and *Jacob,* with innumerable more, it is not therefore difpleafing in God's Sight, that Men fhould have a numerous Progeny: And likewife, though there is feldom much Amity and Peace between Step-Mothers and their Daughters-in-Law, yet is not Matrimony therefore difpleafing to God. So, in like manner, though among diverfe Wives of the fame Hufband there has feldom been good Agreement, yet cannot either Matrimony itfelf in general, or the Marriage of fundry Wives to one Man, be therefore juftly condemned, but only fuch Wives as had not Difpofitions fo good as they fhould have had.

O. Chriftians, in this Life, ought to be Contemners of Pleafures, and to have more of the Spirit than thofe had who lived under the *Old Law.* Wherefore, notwithftanding thofe our Predeceffors had a Plurality of Wives, we ought certainly to be fatisfied with each of us one.

T. It is needlefs I repeat it, having already declared to you my Sentiment, that it is far from being unlawful for a Man

to

to cohabit with a Diverfity of Wives; neither is it any way inconfiftent with the moft elevated Degree of Faith and Perfection. Nor can I comprehend from whence you can be affured, that fome Chriftians have not a Call from the ALMIGHTY to cohabit with fundry Wives, as well as fome of the *Jews* were, by him, heretofore called fo to do.

O. Urge whatever you can, to have a Plurality of Wives is both difhoneft, indecent and filthy.

T. You are dragged into this erroneous Opinion, by two Things. The firft is Cuftom: For if it were cuftomary for Men to have more Wives than one, you would not look on it to be either blameable or unfeemly. The other is a certain hypocritical Sanctity, which induces you to fancy the having more than one Wife to be a Thing unlawful, tho' it is not at all repugnant to Sacred Writ: And fuch as are convicted of having more Wives than one, have far greater Punifhments inflicted on them than would be, fhould they entertain a thoufand Harlots.

O. A Man finds it no eafy Matter to fatisfy one Woman; yet you would have it allowable for him to have a Plurality!

T. A

T. Telypolygamus   *O. Ochinus*

T. A Husband is not bound to satiate all his Wife's Carnal Appetites, but only such as are moderated with Reason.

O. Under the *Old Testament*, when the World was but thinly peopled, it was, perhaps, expedient, that Men should have a Plurality of Wives: But now the Earth is so very populous as it is, there is no manner of Necessity for it.

T. In Answer to that ; first, you are not certain, whether Men, in case they had a Diversity of Wives, would be much more fruitful in Children than they are: Or even if their Offspring (as probably it might) should prove abundantly more numerous, how know you but that the Products of the Earth would be so increased as to afford a Sufficiency for their Nourishment, and all their other Necessities ? For the same GOD, who had so multiplied Mankind, might also increase and multiply the Fruits to a competent Plenty for their Sustenance. But, suppose you were certain, that they would all perish with Want, yet of so high Price are the Souls of Men, that we ought not, by any Means, to prevent their Existence, especially if we are thereunto called by our Creator, as were, of old, those Holy Men who had a Plurality of Wives.

O. In

T. Telypolygamus   *O. Ochinus*

On POLYGAMY.

O. In thefe Days of ours, a *Chriſtan* ſhould not have more than one Wife; if for no other Reaſon, at leaſt to avoid the Scandal and Offence would thence ariſe; ſince all *Chriſtians* look on the having more Wives than one to be a Thing not only moſt deteſtably filthy, but even diabolical.

T. Juſt ſo, as even though the Generality of Men ſhould combine to account Matrimony itſelf to be utterly unlawful and abominable, yet ought not you to regard the Offence it gave them, but to marry, if you had thereunto a Call; ſo ought you alſo to mary more than one, if you were thereunto ſtimulatied by Divine Impulſe.

O. A Single Man, indeed, in ſuch a Caſe might marry, to avoid falling into Uncleanneſs, though Men ſhould take Offence at his ſo doing; eſpecially if he had a Call to it from Above. But he who already has one Wife, has no Need to take another; neither will he be thereunto called by Impulſe Divine.

T. Nay certainly, if his Wife be inrfim, or troubled with any other Impediment, ſo that he cannot have due Enjoyment of her, and he has not the Gift of Continence, he neceſſarily muſt, to avoid Uncleanneſs, marry another. Add to this, that it is not merely

T. Telypolygamus   *O. Ochinus*

merely to avoid Uncleanness that GOD calls Men to marry, but chiefly for Procreation sake, as of old he called *Abraham*, and other Holy Men.

O. Shall I make it clearly manifest to you, that the having more than one Wife is a Thing actually prohibited? *Christ* says; *That if any Man puts away his Wife, except for Adultery, and shall marry another, he commits Adultery.* But if a Man might have more Wives than one, he should not commit Adultery, as *Christ* says, whether he puts away his former Wife, or no.

T. No Man can better expound those Words of *Christ*, than *Christ* himself; who, in another Place, explaining the last Words, says; *Whosoever shall put away his Wife, except for Adultery, causes her to commit Adultery.* That is to say; he gives Occasion to his Wife, so unjustly put away, to commit Adultery: For the Wife being thus deprived of her rightful Husband, cannot, during his Life, espouse any other without being guilty of Adultery. Therefore *Christ* says not; *If any Man puts away his Wife, not for Adultery, and marries another, he commits Adultery*; but that, *he gives his repudiated Wife Occasion to commit Adultery.*

O. Matthew, Mark and *Luke* all record, that *Christ* said; *If any Man puts away his Wife, and marries another, he commits Adultery*;

T. Telypolygamus   *O. Ochinus*

tery; meaning, by marrying that other. But if his Meaning was to shew, that, by his divorcing her unjustly, he gave her Occasion to commit Adultery, it would have been sufficient to have said ; *If any Man puts away his Wife, he commits Adultery*; without adding, *and marries another*. Wherefore *Christ*, by those his Words, in *Matthew* v. designed not to expound that Expression in the said Evangelist, *Chap.* xix; only he said ; *If any Man puts away his Wife, not for Adultery, he makes her commit Adultery*. But, elsewhere, he expresses himself differently ; *viz. That if he marries another, in the same Kind, he commits Adultery:* Because the first only was his Wife, and it was not lawful he should have more than one. To this add, that *Christ*'s Words, in his Sermon upon the Mount, were spoken before those were uttered, by which he answered the *Pharisees*, who asked him ; *Whether a Man, for every Cause, might put away his Wife?* Wherefore those Words cannot be the Exposition of these, which were spoken afterwards,

T. Whether the latter Words were an Exposition of the former, or not, I am satisfied, that both mean one and the same Thing ; *viz. That if any Man shall put away his Wife, without just Cause, he*
occasions

T. Telypolygamus *O. Ochinus*

occasions her to commit Adultery: And as for the additional Words, in Chap. xix, *Christ* added them only to demonstrate, that if a Wife, unjustly divorced, marries another Man, she commits Adultery; tho', at the same Time, her former Husband has married another Woman; since her first Matrimony is not void, but continues in its full Force. *Christ*'s Meaning, is, therefore, this: *If he puts her away without just Cause, tho' he marries another, yet he gives to her, who is so put away, Occasion to commit Adultery.*

O. You so force and strain this your Interpretation, that it is in ths greatest Danger of breaking. Nay, we may also see even irrational Creatures, that each Male has its peculiar Female, with which alone it couples, as in Birds of all Kinds: And much more does it become Men, particularly *Christians*, to do the like.

T. This is Fact only in such Creatures whose Propagation is not of much Necessity towards Man's Sustenance: But, by Observation, you may find one Cock to have many Hens; one Bull many Cows; and

T. Telypolygamus   *O. Ochinus*

and the same in many other Creatures of Utility to Mankind. If, therefore, by Divine Ordinance, and for Man's Benefit, one Cock has many Hens, much more is it the ALMIGHTY's Pleasure, that a Man may have several Women, for the Propagation of Men, whom he so tenderly loves and so highly prizes.

O. Were none of those Creatures, you mention, emasculated by Castration, and were assembled together in great Numbers, you would find each Male with only his own peculiar Female; much more ought it to be so with Men: But, very many of the Males being castrated, and few of the Species together in one Place, if one Male does couple with diverse Females, it does not, therefore, follow, that one Man should have diverse Wives. Into the Ark of *Noah* the ALMIGHTY sent just as many Males as Females, to shew, that each Male should have only his own single Female.

T. I confess, that were the Number of Men and Women in the World exactly equal, it would be very expedient, that each Man should have only a single Wife. But since the Number of Women is far greater, I conceive it to be reasonable for one Man to have diverse Women; for it is not in vain that GOD creates a greater Number of Females, of our Species, than

He

T. Telypolygamus   *O. Ochinus*

He does Males. But, suppose, for Example, there were, in the whole World, only 300 Women, and just as many Men, and every Man had one Woman; they would not so soon propagate their Kind as if 400 of the 600 were Females, and 200 Males, each of which had two Women. And on this Account it is, that GOD is pleased to create more Women than Men: The Life of one Man being equal to those of two Women.

O. Hold! In the first Place, I believe not, that you can be certain of there being more Women in the World than there are Men. You, perhaps, fancy so, because we are apt to rejoice at the Birth of a Boy, and the contrary for a Girl. And even admit, that more Girls are born into the World than Boys, yet the Majority of them are very short-lived, by reason of their tenderer Constitution. Besides, abundance more Men than Women are destroyed by War, Shipwreck, the Sword of Justice, &c. Yet cannot any of all this be a sufficient Plea for, or Proof of the Necessity or Legality of *Polygamy.* And as for the Love of Carnal Society, it is a Passion than which no Passion is more violent: And if even a dishonest Love cannot brook a Partnership, much less may that which is honest and irreproachable!

T. Pious

T. Telypolygamus   *O. Ochinus*

On POLYGAMY.

T. Pious Love rather extends to all Mankind, even to our very Enemies.

O. *Jacob* was a pious, good Man; and yet he loved barren *Rachel* more than fruitful *Leah*: So also did *Helkanah* love barren *Hannah* better than he did *Peninnah*, who was otherwise. *Soloman* likewise said, that his Beloved was *one*. Wherefore it is a very difficult Task for a Man to distribute his Affection and Benevolence, equally and impartially, among several Wives, which, yet, must be done where *Polygamy* is admitted. When a Man has but one Wife, a reciprocal Love is better preserved than if he had a Plurality; and in case of any Quarrel between a Man and his single Wife, they are more easily reconciled. Amidst a Plurality of Wives, contrary Opinions abound, and there never wants a comfortless Scene of Discord and Distraction.

T. Were

> The Fault lies not in *Polygamy*, but in the fractious Dispositions of those discording Females.

T. Telypolygamus *O. Ochinus*

T. Were there a Call from God, their State would not be without the Divine Benediction. *Polygamy* is no Enemy to Concord and Charity. Therefore if a Man has several Wives, and there is no Agreement among them, the Fault lies not in *Polygamy*, but in the fractious Dispositions of those discording Females.

O. If the Filthy Love of a vile Strumpet is, often, the Occasion of a Man's being satisfied with only her, abundantly more should a like Effect be worked by the Sacred Love of Matrimony.

T. We daily see, that some Filthy Love has a better Effect on some, than the Sacred Matrimonial Love has on others; also, in like Manner, Supperstition produces more Good in some, than does True Religion in others; all which is owing to the Instigation and Influence of the Devil.

O. That *Polygamy* is repugnant to Natural Reason is manifest in its being ever abstained from by all Nations, as a Thing not lawful.

T. You are sensible, that the Light of Nature, I mean, that Natural Law which Men have in their Hearts imprinted, is the Gift of God, and that it is just, and that the Law of *Moses* is not contrary to it, but an Explanation thereof: For if the Law of *Moses* were repugnant to the Law of Nature,

T. Telypolygamus   *O. Ochinus*

On POLYGAMY.

ture, GOD would be contrary to Himself, since they both proceed from GOD, or rather both are one and the same Law. Wherefore, if Plurality of Wives had been repugnant to Reason, certainly, neither would *Moses* have connived at it, those holy good *Patriarchs* have practised it, nor the ALMIGHTY have suffered it. When GOD, by *Moses*, commanded the *Israelites*, that when they came upon the Borders of the *Gentiles*, they should not imitate their Vices, He would, among other prohibited Practises, have named *Polygamy*, had it been contrary to Law; and he would, by *Moses*, have forbid it, which he did not: Neither do we any where read, that GOD ever punished any Man for his having Plurality of Wives, nor that by his Prophets, they were even once threatened, on that Account. If you desire to make the Manners of the *Gentiles* your Rule and Law, you will find them abounding in Wickedness. And as to your Assertion, that all Nations abstained from and abhored *Polygamy*, it is a Falsity, as appears in the *Hebrews*: Also *Chremes* had two Wives, if we may credit *Terence*; so had *Boocus*, as we are told by *Sallust*: And, to conclude, so had *Socrates* himself, who, nevertheless, was a most wise Man, and had

a very

a very plentiful Portion of the Light of Nature.

O. Even the wifeſt of Men ſometimes err.

T. None did ever condemn, or reprehend *Socrates*, on Account of his *Bygamy*, or having two Wives, tho' he has been much cenſured on other Accounts. But why ſhould we uſe Multiplicity of Arguments? *Polygamy* was, and ſtill is, practiſed as a beneficial Cuſtom, moſt profitable to Mankind by advancing Propagation, not only among the *Jews*, but likewiſe by the *Perſians*, *Turks*, and others. In *Europe* only it is deemed abominable; in which *Europe*, Vice has abounded, and ſtill does, if not more, yet not one Jot leſs, than in any other Part of the Univerſe. Nay, in former Ages, *Polygamy* has been favourably looked on even in *Europe*; only they avoided having, in one Houſe, more than one Miſtreſs of the Family, which was a Piece of Prudence, as being very convenient to prevent Noiſe and Confuſion.

O. Well, but what ſay you to the *Imperial* Laws, which make quite againſt you?

T. Whereabouts, pray, is that?

O. Firſt of all, the Emperors *Diocleſianus* and *Maximinus*, abſolutely prohibit *Polygamy*, in theſe Words: *That no Man, within the Juriſdiction of the* Roman *Empire,*

can

T. Telypolygamus   *O. Ochinus*

On POLYGAMY.

can have two Wives: Since, also, in the Prætorian *Edict, such Men are branded with Infamy; which Delinquency no equitable Judge will suffer to pass with Impunity.* The same *Code* likewise says: *Undoubtedly, the Man who has two Wives, is not free from Infamy.*

T. You say, the Authors of the first *Imperial* Law were *Dioclesianus* and *Maximinus:* The other is taken from a *Rescript* of the Emperors *Valerianus* and *Galienus.*

O. It suffices, that being Emperors, they were invested with the Power of enacting Laws.

T. We must not forget, that, in the *Pagan* Empire, such was the Matrimonial Constitution, that, for any light and frivolous Cause, Men might turn off their Wives, and entertain Harlots at Discretion, without much Reproach: Yet had not such Concubines either the Name or Authority of Wives. On this Account the Emperors made those Decrees, not because they deemed *Polygamy* to be unlawful, seeing they allow a Plurality of legal Concubines; but they judged it reasonable, that the first alone should bear the Title and Privileges of a Wife; more particularly, since the Man might part with her if she suited him not.

D 2 *O.* But

T. Telypolygamus   *O. Ochinus*

O. But we see, that the Emperor *Constantinus* prohibited all Concubinage.

T. If you weigh well his Words, you will comprehend, that his Intention was only to inhibit him who had a Wife to entertain Concubines; not that the having them was actually illegal, but a Man was not to have them with him in the House where his Wife was; and this merely to prevent Contention and Disquiet: But separately, every Man might have as many as he pleased. And the Emperor *Valentinianus*, invested with a like Power and Authority, did not only permit such as had Wives to keep Concubines, but many Wives also at the same Time, and in the same House, all dignified with the same Title, and bearing equal Authority: The said Emperor himself, also had a Diversity of Wives. Now this Law of *Valentinianus*, which was of a later Date than that of *Constantinus*, did intirely abrogate the same, so that it became void.

O. Justinianus makes not any Mention, in his *Code*, of this Law of *Valentinianus*.

T. Nevertheless, it undoubtedly was publickly recorded, as we are informed in History. To this we may add, that, besides, this Emperor, it is well known, that *Constantius*, Son of *Constantinus*, had sundry Wives. Likewise *Clotarius*, King of *France*, and

On POLYGAMY.

and *Heribertus* and *Hypericus*, his Sons, had a Diverſity of Wives. I add alſo, *Pipinus* and *Carolus Magnus*, of whom *Urſpergenſis* witneſſes, that they had each more than one Wife: Nay, we may, likewiſe, add *Arnulphus* and *Fredericus Barbaroſſa*, both Emperors of *Germany*, with *Philippus Deodatus*, King of *France*, and innumerable others. Not that I will deny, but that it is abominably criminal in thoſe who, abandoning their Wives, go into foreign Countries, and there marry others: I only ſpeak in Behalf of thoſe well diſpoſed Men who, ſuppoſing the ALMIGHTY *calls* them to a Diverſity of Wives, are mindful to maintain and cheriſh them all, as they ought to do.

O. You are ſuppoſing what never yet was in the Creation, which is, That GOD ever *called* a Man to a Diverſity of Wives.

T. Certainly, *Abraham*, *Jacob*, and an Infinity of others, were thereunto called by the LORD; and, doubtleſs, the like may be with us. Nor can I ſee, what more Need had they of ſuch a *Call* than we have; or why it was more their Duty than ours, to raiſe a numerous Progeny.

O. The Emperor *Conſtantinus* would not allow a Plurality of Wives, nor will the preſent reigning Emperor.

T. My

T. Telypolygamus *O. Ochinus*

T. My Inquiry is after what is equitable and expedient, and not after what Men in Power will, or will not. Nature's Laws are immutable: And if, in *Abraham*'s Time, it was confonant to Reafon to have Diverfity of Wives, and deemed a Matter neither difhoneft nor unjuft (for if it had, we may be affured, that good Patriarch would not have taken to his Bed more than one) we muft confefs it to be, now, in our Days, likewife juft, honeft and expedient; and fo it was in the Days of *Conftantinus*: For, notwithftanding his Imperial Authority, he could not make that to be indecent and unjuft, which in itfelf was juft and honourable. Undoubtedly, that ancient Church of *Chrift* had the Knowledge of Divine Matters; and yet, neither that Church, nor the Emperors of thofe Times, did condemn or punifh *Polygamy*. But Men had rather *feem to be good*, than *be fo indeed*; feeing they fo furioufly cry-down a Diverfity of Wives, yet are fuch Lovers of Adultery and Fornication. Finally, to condemn *Polygamy*, is for Man to prefer himfelf to GOD, who never did condemn it, and to affume a greater Degree of Perfection than He. I fpare faying, that I may not allow of the Laws of the Emperors, in Matrimonial Cafes; feeing

On POLYGAMY.

ing they refer those Matters to the Ecclesiastical Laws.

O. If by them you will be tryed, I am Victor.

T. Produce me one *Canon* which makes for you.

O. In the Times of the *Fathers* of the Church, *Polygamy* was accounted so notoriously filthy and abominable, that they did not think it fitting to condemn it expresly by Words.

T. Now I, for my Part, am verily persuaded, that those Fathers of the ancient Church were contented with the *Canon* of St. *Paul*, who would have those who were Ministers of the Church to be satisfied with one Wife; not on account of its being in itself illegal to have more, but that they might the better attend and execute their Function: But, as for all others, he allowed them to do, in that Case, according to the *inward Motions* they had from *Above*.

O. We know that, in the third and seventh *Neocæsariensian* Councils, *Polygamy* was prohibited.

T. I assert, that it never was prohibited, neither in those *Councils*, nor in any other.

O. Certain I am, that they ordained a Penalty for *Polygamists*; which never would have been done, had they not judged it illegal

T. Telypolygamus *O. Ochinus*

illegal for a Man to have more than one Wife: Nay, they forbad all Priests to be present at the Marriages of those who would have more Wives than one.

T. Right; they did so: But at the same Time, they did not forbid *Polygamy* itself.

O. They sufficiently forbad it, when they ordained Punishments for it.

T. Should you read through every one of the *Councils*, you will not therein find *Polygamy* to be prohibited. Neither can that be alledged as the Reason, because they conceived *it* to be forbid in Scripture: Since I have already demonstrated *its* not being there inhibited. And, in *Canon* 17 of the *Apostles*, it is decreed; *That a Man, having two Wives, should be removed from the* Episcopal *and* Priestly Function, *and from all other* Ecclesiastical *Offices*. But had the Authors of those *Canons* looked upon *Polygamy* itself to have been repugnant to Scripture, *Christian*-Charity, and the common Good of Mankind, they, assuredly, would have Excommunicated all those who had more than one Wife; nor would they only have banished such Men from their Communion, but would, likewise, have inflicted on them grievous Corporal Punishments. But those Apostolical Fathers, as *Paul* had done before them, forbad

On POLYGAMY.

had only the Ministers of the Church to have more Wives than one; not as if it was a Thing contrary to *Christian* and Moral Honesty, but because it would draw away and divert them from Spiritual Exercises. But because, in Process of Time, Men began, by Degrees, to turn aside from the Right Way, so that many fell to account even Matrimony itself to be unlawful; they blushed not to give it under their Hands, *That a Man's first Wife being dead, it was* Adultery, *and not* Marriage, *to take another:* Touching which Matters, you may see much in *Gratianus*. So do, likewise, *Hieronimus* and *Tertullianus* interpret that Saying of *Paul* and the *Apostles*, as if the Meaning and Intention was; *That he who had two Wives, though successively, might not be admitted a* Minister *of* Christ's *Church; neither he who espoused a Widow, or a Divorced Wife:* All which we know to be still in Force among many. And, among the *Reverend* of the *Romish* Creed, we see, that Matrimony, in any Sort or Degree, is utterly thrown out of Doors; tho' we daily see Persons, most *Sir-Reverendly* noted for Filthiness, promoted to their chiefest Church Dignities! But mark what I am about to advance. The Life of a Courtier, and a Soldier, cannot be deemed really sinful *in Terminis*, but many may be thereunto called

T. Telypolygamus   *O. Ochinus*

called by GOD Himself: Yet, in the 12th *Canon* of the *Nicene* Council, it was decreed ; *That those who having once quitted the Profession of Arms, and again went to the Wars, should be severely punished* ; tho', in those Days, seldom any War was moved, except against Infidels and Idolaters. In like Manner, tho' they decreed Penalties for such as had two Wives, yet is not *Bigamy* therefore sinful, but many be thereunto called by Instinct Divine. There are abundance of such *Canons*, particularly touching Matrimony, which want Amendment ; not that we are tied by any *Canons*, but such only as have their Foundations on the Word of GOD. The *Fathers* have many Times erred, as being Men, and not unfrequently swerving from the Rule of GOD's Word. Moreover, we ought to believe, that *Paul* taught (for Example) the *Ephesians*, and the rest of the Churches, all Things necessary to Salvation ; as himself testifies : And yet he taught them not, that any were to be *tied to one Wife*, excepting Ministers of the Church.

O. That he might, perhaps, do, to the Intent that, by their Example, others might, by little and little, be brought to a like laudable Practise.

T. In the first Place, what you urge is not grounded on any Part of GOD's Injunctions ;

T. Telypolygamus   *O. Ochinus*

On POLYGAMY.   59

junctions; without which, according to my Sentiments, it is no less than Impiety to force or bind Consciences. Nor ought every Thing which is expedient for a Bishop, to be propounded as a Model for all others to copy after.

O. Yet, it is a bold Word for us to say, that the Church has erred, now, for upwards of Twelve Hundred Years, in condemning and punishing *Bigamy*.

T. That Error is not to be attributed to GOD's Church, but to Men; who, in the Church, have as much erred in prohibiting Marriage to Priests: Yea, and I would have you take Notice, that the *Neocæsariensian* Council did not decree, that *the Second Wife should be divorced*; nor that *the Second was no true Marriage*.

O. The Council sufficiently declared that, by decreeing Penalties for such as had two Wives.

T. Augustinus judges that Man *to be guilty of Sin who marries, after having made a Vow of Chastity:* And yet he accounts such to be a *true Marriage*, and that the same *ought not to be made void*. This Argument is not, therefore, of any Force or Validity: The Council enacted Penalties for such as had two Wives; and therefore the Second was not a true Marriage. Moreover, tho' more than a Thousand Years are passed since Penalties

nalties were enacted for those who had two Wives, yet it is not above Four Hundred Years since that Decree was first received by the *Italians, Spaniards,* and *Germans.* And as for the Institution, it is merely Human; and the Bishops would have exclaimed against the Emperor *Valentinianus,* for his Plurality of Wives, but that he had Scripture on his Side: And, notwithstanding they reprehended such as had more than one Wife, as *Augustinus* and *Bonifacius* did, as Persons who seemed over-indulgent to the Flesh, yet they did not, therefore, Excommunicate them, or deem them among the Number of such as could not be Saved. *Ambrosius* was a very sharp Reprover of Sin; yet we do not any-where read, that he reproved *Valentinianus* for having a Diversity of Wives: Yea, and the said *Ambrosius,* reprehending his second Wife, *Justina,* for her *Arianism,* ought withal to have reprehended her for not being a true Wife, but a Concubine; which, notwithstanding, he did not do. It is, likewise, recorded, that *Leo* V. when he understood, that a certain Bishop, in *Africa,* had two Wives, he only decreed, that, by reason of the Words of *Paul, he should be degraded and deprived of his Office?* but not that *he should be obliged to divorce his Second Wife,* or *be any other Way punished on account*

count of his Bigamy. *Gregorius*, also Bishop of *Rome*, writing to *Bonifacius*, who was sent into *Germany* to teach *Christianity*, a Hundred and Twenty Years after *Christ*'s Nativity, beseeches him, *To take Care, that such as had espoused a Plurality of Women, and had buried all except one, might content themselves with that one, and not take any other.* So that he only exhorts Men to abstain from *Polygamy*, just as he might exhort them to *Celibacy*; which cannot be understood of any but of such as are, by the ALMIGHTY, called to that State of Life. The true Ecclesiastical *Canons*, which oblige us to their Observance, are such as are grounded on the Divine Word. But, to convince you, read the Epistle written by *Gregorius* III. Bishop of *Rome*, to the above-cited *Bonifacius*, where you shall find him saying to this Purpose, *viz.*

If any Man has a Wife, who, by reason of some bodily Infirmity, cannot afford to her Husband due Benevolence, he shall do well to abstain from her: But if he cannot contain *(for that is the Gift of* GOD, *not given to all) it is better he should marry another Wife, than* burn; *provided he allows his former Wife all necessary Maintenance.*——
Than which, what can be more clearly expressed?

O. All

T. Telypolygamus　　　　　*O. Ochinus*

O. All you can utter, should you plead till *Dooms-Day*, will never convince me, that it is either decent, reasonable, or lawful for a Man to have more than a single Wife.

T. Set the Case, that the Number of Women does every where exceed that of the Men, What must become of the poor un-mated Women?

O. They must take the same Course as the Men should do, if the Number of Men exceeded: That is: Pray to GOD to bestow on them the Gift of *Continence*.

T. In case GOD calls, to a Married State, a Man who has not the least Portion of that *Gift* of *Continence*, so requisite to a Single Life, it would be but in vain for him to pray for the *Gift* of being rendered able to live without a Wife; for I am of Opinion, he would not obtain his Request, since GOD calls him to marry.

O. The whole [*Christian*] World has believed *Polygamy* to be unlawful; nor can any Man have more than one Wife, without giving all imaginable Offence, which by all ought carefully to be avoided. Besides, GOD wills us, *to be obedient to our Magistrates:* And they are so far from allowing *Polygamy*, that they will put to Death the Man who is proved to have two Wives.

T. But

T. Telypolygamus   *O. Ochinus*

T. But not, if he keeps about him a whole Troop of Whores! ——— If any Man, being, by Instinct Divine, moved to marry diverse Women, and his so doing should be no Sin, if he married them, it were (as the *Schools* speak) a *Scandal taken*, and not *given*. Also, to avoid Scandal, he might marry his Second Wife privately.

O. Such Matters are, however, scarcely practicable: And if he should be seen frequently in his Second Wife's Company, the World would take Offence, as judging her to be his Concubine. I shall therefore, continually persevere in exhorting Men to shun *Polygamy*; and I heartily dehort you from thinking on it. Even the *Romish* Clergy make Vows of perpetual *Celibacy*: And shall we, who are Men Regenerate, Spiritual and Evangelical, think of entertaining a Diversity of Wives!

T. Right! And how chastly those Single-Livers pass their vowed *Celibacy*, all the World knows, and observes. The Law itself condemns *unfruitful Matrimony*; so far is it from not condemning spontaneous *unfruitful Celibacy*. Now, I speak expresly of such as are not called to a *Single Life*. The ancient *Romans* used to punish those who lived unmarried, and rewarded such as augmented the Common-Weal by

T. Telypolygamus　　　　*O. Ochinus*

a numerous Progeny. The like was also decreed by *Lycurgus* and *Ulpianus*. Now, what can merit a greater Benediction than the Preservation of Mankind, which, were it not for Matrimony, would be utterly annihilate ? A Man cannot transmit to Posterity a more honourable Memorial of his Name, than by leaving behind him Children virtuously educated. And what greater Folly can be imagined, than, under a Shew of Holiness, to shun Holy Matrimony, as a Thing profane, which, nevertheless, has been ordained by GOD; is dictated by *Nature*; is persuaded by *Reason*; was confirmed by *Christ*; has been, and is, praised by *Writers*, Sacred and Profane; authorized by all *Laws*; unanimously approved by all *Nations*! and whereunto we are invited by the Example of the best *Men* ? On the other Hand; What more inhumanly barbarous, than to hate Matrimony, the Desire whereof we have in us implanted by Nature ? What more ungratefully unthankful to Nature, the World, and our own Species, than not to beget Children, as our Ancestors and Parents have begot Us ? For my Part, I make Account, that such Men are Murderers of as many as they might have begotten had they embraced Matrimony; except, peradventure, they are carried by

a

a Divine Impulse to lead a Single Life. Queſtionleſs, it is a Sort of Man-Slaughter, not only to cauſe Abortion or Sterility by Drugs, or the like, but alſo to ſhun Matrimony, without very juſt Cauſe.

O. I am not condemning Matrimony, namely, the having one Wife; but the having two, or more.

T. But what is it you will adviſe me to?

O. To think no more of marrying any more Wives, but to pray to GOD for the *Gift* of *Continency.*

T. What, if he will not give *it* me;

O. He will, if you pray in *Faith.*

T. What, if He neither gives me the *Gift*, nor the *Faith* to aſk *it?*

O. If you then do that to which GOD ſhall incline you, ſo that you are ſure that you are led by Divine Inſtigation, you ſhall not err. For it can be no Error to obey GOD. Other Advice I cannot give you. Therefore, I bid you *Farewel*; and promiſe you, that I will ſeek the LORD in your Behalf.

T. And that is what I beſeech you to do, that I may not offend GOD; but that I may give him all Honour and Glory, thro' CHRIST our LORD, *Amen.*

F I N I S.

T. Telypolygamus   *O. Ochinus*

Dialog on Polygamy - Edited by Don Milton

Other Books Published by Don Milton

Title	Author	Availability
Prince of Sumba Husband to Many Wives	Don Milton	Now
Letters to Joseph Priestley	Martin Madan	Now
Exhortatory Address to the Brethren in the Faith of Christ	Martin Madan	Now
Thelyphthora Volume I A Treatise on Female Ruin	Martin Madan	Now
Thelyphthora Volume II A Treatise on Female Ruin	Martin Madan	Now
Thelyphthora Volume III A Treatise on Female Ruin	Martin Madan	Now
Juvenal and Persius Volume I	Martin Madan	
Juvenal and Persius Volume II	Martin Madan	Now
Thoughts on Executive Justice	Martin Madan	May 2009
John Milton on Polygamy	John Milton	May 2009
Many More Titles	Don Milton & Others	Fall 2009

To Purchase Books or to Contact Don Milton
Visit - DonMilton.com or write:

Don Milton
PO Box 10162
Scottsdale, AZ 85271-0162

www.ingramcontent.com/pod-product-compliance
Lightning Source LLC
Chambersburg PA
CBHW031253290426
44109CB00012B/568